'Being born and raised in a conflict zone as a ... s made peace and actively seeking peace a fundamental part of my life as a Christian. Reading David's book, I was immediately encouraged, inspired and challenged by it. Shalom is proactive, and living it out and sharing it should be at the core of who we are. Read this amazing book and be as challenged as I was to make a difference in the world in which we live.'

Tanas Al Qassis, Regional Manager for Europe, the Middle East and North Africa, CMS

'Insightful, challenging and impactful – *The Prince of Peace in a World of Wars* reframes the traditional Christian doctrines into the biblical theme of shalom and reiterates that theme in the light of the personal journeys undertaken by biblical characters. In so doing the book gently yet firmly bids us to collide into our violent times with the truth of Christ Jesus the Prince of Peace, only to make his peace, hope and care tangible wherever and whenever in the power of the Spirit. This book reminds us that peace is doable and worthy of our pursuit!'

Miyon Chung, Lecturer in Christian Thought, Morling College, Sydney, Australia

'Drawing on decades of service as a pastor, mission worker and global Baptist leader, David has produced a wise, insightful and tender book that carries the air of authenticity. Its enduring themes have a timeless wisdom, making this a book to go back to again and again.'

Mark Craig, Director of Communications, BMS World Mission

The Bible Reading Fellowship
15 The Chambers, Vineyard
Abingdon OX14 3FE
brf.org.uk

The Bible Reading Fellowship (BRF) is a Registered Charity (233280)

ISBN 978 0 85746 570 2
First published 2018
10 9 8 7 6 5 4 3 2 1 0
All rights reserved

Acknowledgements
Unless otherwise stated, scripture quotations are taken from The New Revised
Standard Version of the Bible, Anglicised edition, copyright © 1989, 1995 by the
Division of Christian Education of the National Council of the Churches of Christ in the
United States of America. Used by permission. All rights reserved.

Scripture quotations marked NIV are taken from The Holy Bible, New International
Version (Anglicised edition) copyright © 1979, 1984, 2011 by Biblica. Used by
permission of Hodder & Stoughton Publishers, an Hachette UK company. All rights
reserved. 'NIV' is a registered trademark of Biblica. UK trademark number 1448790

Every effort has been made to trace and contact copyright owners for material used
in this resource. We apologise for any inadvertent omissions or errors, and would
ask those concerned to contact us so that full acknowledgement can be made in the
future.

A catalogue record for this book is available from the British Library

Printed and bound by CPI Group (UK) Ltd, Croydon CR0 4YY

David Kerrigan

The
Prince of Peace
in a World
of Wars

Applying the message of
God's love to a needy world

For Janet
my companion on the way
and for the BMS World Mission family
who gave us the opportunity to be peacemakers

Contents

Introduction

The Prince of Peace in a world of wars

Every Christmas we take the seasonal decorations from the attic, and among them is a candle adorned with the titles given to Jesus. One of those is Prince of Peace, and the purpose of this book is to ask what that title means and how its promise can be real for us and for the world in which we live.

I love mobiles. Not the phones but the kind that we hang over a baby's cot to provide something of interest for the infant as they begin to get to grips with this strange world into which they have arrived. Left alone, the mobile will achieve a state of equilibrium, but a puff of air, a small vibration or a sideways swipe will destroy the balance.

Is that a picture of what peace is? For sure, peace *can be* an experience of stillness, but if we want our lives to be peaceful – literally full of peace – we need something more fluid, more adaptable, something that is with us when the pieces are moving, when life is fast and uncertain, when problems emerge unpredictably from left and right. We need something that is dynamic not stationary, fluid not rigid, as we ride the rollercoaster of the joys and the storms of life.

My earliest memory of a disturbance of the peace was me cuddling my one-year-old baby brother, arms wrapped around him, genuinely worrying whether our family life was about to be destroyed by a nuclear war. If that seems fanciful, just the product of a febrile imagination, let me tell you that the year was 1962, I was eight years old and the Cuban missile crisis held the world in its grip. Each day brought new developments, but the atmosphere was palpably tense, even to an eight-year-old. These were not the days of 24-hour news, so gathering round the radio or the recently acquired black-and-white TV was an anxious experience. We needed to know what had changed from yesterday or last night. Even at that young age I was taking in everything, and I was scared.

The year 2018 marks the centenary of the end of World War I, supposedly 'the day the guns fell silent'. But they haven't been silent for long, and in the years since there have been countless wars that continue to this day. Understandably, we ask whether we will ever see a world at peace.

But not all wars are between armies. There are the wars that tear relationships apart. Once-lifelong friends argue and stop speaking to each other for years. Children grow up and flex their muscles and distance themselves from their once-revered parents, who now can only look on and feel the pain of unexpected rebellion. Elsewhere, wives and husbands rage over matters great and small. In the silence of the night they weep and ache in equal measure and whisper to themselves in the outgoing breath, 'How did it come to this?' They fight daily battles, often against their better intentions, but they don't know how to stop. They've become utterly lost and cannot find the way back. They're not even sure they want to.

Even closer to home, there's the battle inside each one of us. The polished exterior that we present to the world masks a multitude of contradictions. Fears, addictions, guilt and bad memories have moved in over the years and taken up residence, invading the space we'd rather reserve for that elusive thing we call peace.

For a moment's respite, we turn on the TV but find no solace for the soul. Within our nation we see stresses and strains that bubble over and destroy whatever semblance of peace we thought existed. The 'haves and have-nots', the unemployed and the unseen decision-makers, desperate migrants and troubled hosts. Wherever difference exists, tensions can rise and explode in our faces. Trouble erupts as sections of society reach breaking point, giving tangible expression to Martin Luther King's declaration that 'a riot is the language of the unheard'.

I'm aware that the canvas I'm painting here is a gloomy one, so let me add quickly that this is only a part of the picture. Most of life's experiences, for most people, are nowhere near as negative. Instead we can recall times of great pleasure around the table with friends, enjoying good food and conversation, or meeting up with pals for a drink where for once we feel we can really be ourselves. And while family life is rarely perfect, it often brings great pleasure. There are joyful moments around birthdays, weddings or holidays, surprise visits and seasonal gatherings that will be remembered in later years when photos are found, memories are shared and the details are willingly exaggerated like the fisherman's daily catch.

Most of our memories will be of ordinary times, of a spring afternoon walk or the light of the weakening sun hitting the golden autumn leaves. These things come and go almost unnoticed, but over the years they make up the sweet normality that life depends on, and if the balance tips in their favour our lives are happy ones and we can speak of the peace that we enjoy. It is these experiences that evoke a fragrance of peace. They are net contributors to the common good, and the peace they create is the gift we crave – the gift we'd cling to if we could only grasp it. I describe this peace as a fragrance, because part of its nature is that it's not tangible; it's elusive. It's not an object that we can pick up and hold, let alone refuse to release.

As we shall see shortly, the disciples who were with Jesus on the night before he died experienced this deep-seated disquiet, and they were afraid. Jesus' response will be our starting point in this quest, and as we will see peace is actually within our grasp. But first we will need to understand what it really is, what it means, what it encompasses. Then we will want to learn from the saints of scripture how they found a measure of peace in trying circumstances. Maybe then we will be in a position to consider the disciplines that can take us to that place of peace we long for, and hold us there, long enough to build a more peaceful world for others.

Along the way, we shouldn't be surprised to see that right at the heart of this story is the birth of a child. There's a degree of irony here, of course, for the birth of a child in some ways fractures the peace of a household – the midnight crying and the incessant demands for attention. Perhaps here we glimpse a truth that will become more apparent as we move on, and priceless too: the peace of God is most needed, and most real, in the midst of turmoil.

A few practical matters to note as we get started. First, the passages I've chosen build a story, but they are not in chronological order. We will first explore that final evening that Jesus spent with his disciples, then dive back to the early pages of the Old Testament, and so on. But gradually I hope that an amazing picture will emerge that will encourage us to see that peace is the very essence, and goal, of the mission of God.

Second, each day will begin with a suggested passage to read. Where the text to be read is too long to be reproduced in full, such as the reading for 1 December, then the verse reference will say, for example, 'Read John 14:22–31' followed by a short extract. Where the text to be read is reproduced in full, as in the reading for 2 December, then the verse reference is simply given (for example, John 14:15–20) followed by the whole passage.

And last, as you're probably reading this book as a devotional aid, do more than read it for information. Read it with an open heart towards God, that he might grant you his peace in the very parts of your life where you need to know it most.

Part I

Understanding peace

1 December

Living with our fears

Read JOHN 14:22–31

> **Peace I leave with you; my peace I give you. I do not give to you as the world gives. Do not let your hearts be troubled, and do not let them be afraid.**
>
> v. 27

Welcome to the beginning. It isn't the beginning in a chronological sense, but it is the beginning of our journey of understanding. We've joined the story towards the end of the earthly life of Jesus. His disciples have travelled with him and learned to trust and love him. They have occasionally puzzled over his teachings, and some have left the group. Over the years together they have seen miracles and observed how different and mysterious this man is. They will have laughed a lot, talked much as they walked along the highways and byways, wondered who he was late into the night and gradually come to that place where all their hopes and dreams are invested in him. They sense he may even be the Messiah, though they can hardly bring themselves to say it. So here are the loyal, faithful, hopeful ones, moments after Judas Iscariot has slipped out into the night.

The mood has been strange all evening. They have been celebrating Passover together, and we're told that Jesus knew his hour had come (John 13:1). No doubt the disciples read something unsettling into Jesus' mood. He has just washed their feet and told them that they should do the same – to serve and not be served is so important. He has hinted – more than hinted – that there was a traitor among them (John 13:21): a strange thing to do, but Jesus had done many strange things over the years.

Jesus spoke of Peter's forthcoming denial, and this will have added to a sense of foreboding. If this was a movie, we would hear the rumbling of thunder in the distance, and an occasional flash of lightning to heighten the tension. If you asked them what was on their minds, the disciples might have quoted Job 3:26: 'I have no peace, no quietness; I have no rest, but only turmoil' (NIV).

The disciples are scared.

Recognising this, Jesus seeks to calm their anxiety. 'Do not let your hearts be troubled,' he says (John 14:1), an unmistakable confirmation that they were indeed *very* troubled. He speaks of the Holy Spirit who will come, elsewhere called the comforter, and then he adds the most enigmatic of statements: 'Peace I leave with you; my peace I give to you. I do not give to you as the world gives. Do not let your hearts be troubled, and do not let them be afraid' (v. 27).

What did he mean by this? What does it mean to have *his* peace? Are there *other* sources of peace? And, strangest of all, what did he mean by 'I do not give to you as the world gives'?

Here, you see, is why this a good place to begin. It's the moment when Jesus spoke most clearly about peace, and in these few words he acknowledges that fear robs us of peace – fear of the known and the unknown; rational fears and irrational ones; big things and small things. But in some mysterious sense, he offers an experience of peace that he himself says is not like the peace you get anywhere else. What kind of peace is he talking about?

Before we address that, let's explore briefly what the absence of peace might look like.

Maybe as you read this you can remember going through a time of illness or depression, or maybe you're going through that today. Living longer is a blessing in many ways, but some of us fear dying. Maybe there are tensions in your marriage or in your relationship with your children, parents or friends. Perhaps it's debt that imposes a weight on you that feels crushing. For others, it's the ache in the stomach from being alone. We crave love and affection; we long for the experience of simply being hugged or touched, yet for some that is elusive. Maybe you're carrying a guilty secret – sometimes we hate these things and love them in equal measure – and we fear the consequences of being found out.

Away from ourselves, switch on the news and we sometimes hear nothing but a litany of woes. Crime is always there in some guise. Terrorism too. Racism and hate rear their ugly heads. Nation rises against nation, and a whole generation of young people have their futures wiped out. If you were an ordinary Syrian family, what would peace look like for you? Or if your fears were for your children as they go to play on the streets of your estate, where drug dealers frequent the darkened stairwells, what would peace look like for you? When you think about climate change and the deep anxiety we have for the generations to come, what would peace look like in that area?

These are just some of the sources, the tip of the iceberg, of our unease. You may be reading this today and in your heart you have an ache that comes from another experience. For you, for most of us, this is all too real.

Peace, I suggest, could simply be the absence of these things, the elimination of that which breaks into our lives and brings fear, anxiety and turmoil. We long for these things to be taken away, and there is nothing wrong in this. Nothing shallow. We often know what robs us of a lightness of spirit, and we want to be rid of it.

These are examples of mostly external factors that affect our sense of peace, but there are others. Many would speak of an inner disquiet, a longing for something deeper, more meaningful and that connects to the spiritual dimension of who they are. Though it's a simplistic picture, the idea of a God-shaped gap in some people's lives illustrates well this yearning.

A moment ago I asked, 'Are there other sources of peace?', and of course the answer for some of the above is yes. This is where, as Christians, we need to be wise in our words and not pretend that the world in which we live has nothing to offer. If our fear is caused by sickness, we need a doctor. If we long for companionship, we want someone to love. Money owed? A windfall wouldn't go amiss. A strained relationship? Let us be reconciled. These things are not just what we crave, but if they come, they work, at least to some degree. We might call these things therapeutic solutions, and they are not to be dismissed.

I stress this because we must not be lazy and write off the world as a no-hope place that at best serves only as heaven's waiting room. We should have no time for a defective theology that refuses to see that God's purposes for the thriving of human life can be fulfilled in part through the gifts and skills he blesses us with as human beings.

But all therapeutic solutions have their limits. Some problems can't be solved. The obvious remedy isn't forthcoming. There isn't an easy answer. And even if one intrusion into our lives is eradicated, there will be something else along in due course. One day we'll all breathe our last, and our life will end. For many people, these scenarios breed fear.

So the really big question is 'Where is a different kind of peace to be found?' A peace that can surmount what seems insurmountable – we might even call it a peace that passes all understanding!

It's to this we turn next.

2 December

The presence of God

JOHN 14:15–20 (NIV)

> 'If you love me, keep my commands. And I will ask the Father, and he will give you another advocate to help you and be with you for ever – the Spirit of truth. The world cannot accept him, because it neither sees him nor knows him. But you know him, for he lives with you and will be in you. I will not leave you as orphans; I will come to you. Before long, the world will not see me any more, but you will see me. Because I live, you also will live. On that day you will realise that I am in my Father, and you are in me, and I am in you.'

With the resurgence of Celtic spirituality in recent years, there has been a renewed interest in the intricate, intertwining artwork that seeks to express the mutual indwelling of the God who is Father, Son and Holy Spirit. Each design weaves in and out, without beginning or end.

We cannot pretend to fully understand what it means to say that God is three-in-one, but the scriptures clearly reveal that the God who is love not only exists in community but *is* community. As Christians, we cannot envisage God other than in the unending, unstarting, interdependent coexistence that we call Trinity. This is often referred to as *perichoresis*, a Greek word that evokes a dance-like movement of weaving in and out; a single entity yet comprising three individual entities. And in this movement we see community – a community of mutual giving and receiving; a community of love, hence John's description that 'God is love' (1 John 4:8).

But as if that was not enough, we are also invited to participate in this divine dance. We can spell it out like this:

- Jesus will ask the Father and he will send the Holy Spirit (v. 16).
- The Holy Spirit will be with you forever (v. 16) and will be in you (v. 17), and you are in Jesus (v. 20) and Jesus is in the Father (v. 20).

In the face of the fear of the apostles, Jesus promises them his peace and this peace is expressed and made real by the indwelling of the Holy Spirit. Through the Holy Spirit we are in Christ and Christ is in the Father (see Colossians 3:3).

In times of trouble or anxiety, it is good to face that situation with a friend or a loved one. There is no doubt some validity in the saying that 'a problem shared is a problem halved' or 'a friend in (my time of) need is a friend indeed'. But the companionship of one another is not the same as the presence of God. The peace that we read of in the Bible, the peace that Jesus speaks of, is not simply the chumminess of friends. If it was then Jesus would have said to his disciples on the night of the Passover, 'Why are you all so glum? Cheer up – you have each other!'

The fear of the disciples is that Jesus is leaving them. The peace he offers is that he is staying. Later, he makes this even more explicit:

> But because I have said these things to you, sorrow has filled your hearts. Nevertheless, I tell you the truth: it is to your advantage that I go away, for if I do not go away, the Advocate will not come to you; but if I go, I will send him to you.
> JOHN 16:6–7

And a few verses later, in John 16:33, he says again, 'I have said this to you, so that in me you may have peace.'

Perhaps here we are beginning to understand what peace means to those who have faith. Christ offers the peace that holds us safe amid the crisis, gives us strength to stand while the storm rages, and carries us through until, perhaps, the problem passes or is resolved, or ultimately until we find our healing in him.

The peace he gives us is his real presence with us. This peace brings about a change in the circumstances of the one who trusts in him, which is why he goes on to say, 'Do not let your hearts be troubled, and do not let them be afraid' (John 14:27). This is why the apostle Paul later refers to the peace Jesus offers as that 'which surpasses all understanding' (Philippians 4:7). 'The Lord is near', Paul says in Philippians 4:5, but of course those who do not believe can't see this; they can't experience it, hence they can't understand it.

This, then, is the secret we will explore in this book: how the presence of God in our lives can be experienced and how it offers us a peace that is beyond measure. This is a most precious gift. This is why the birth of Jesus is of the utmost importance to us, and to the world.

Before we move on, however, let me add a word about what I have called therapeutic solutions that bring peace. As we saw yesterday, the world and its wonderful people will at times be able to ease or even remove our problem. In this book I want to hold together both the goodness of this fallen world, which can still contribute to our peace and well-being, and the absolute necessity of a relationship with God, whose peace is unimaginably different from that which the world can offer.

But if the peace that comes from our human endeavour – the healing, prevention, cure and companionship – is of value, then these things are not just to be celebrated but encouraged. We live our lives as embodied people, and what robs us of peace is the absence of food and water, clothing and shelter, health and education, justice and security. The Bible has no space for a 'peace' that ignores these things, saying in effect 'life may be awful but it's okay because we have Jesus'. A cursory glance at Matthew 25:31–46 tells us that Jesus cared about life's necessities being available to everyone, especially 'the least of these'. Yes, the presence of Jesus has sustained countless souls in the most awful circumstances, but that is no excuse for inaction in the face of injustice. If the goal of God's kingdom is the restoration of God's peace, then the mission of the church must aim to restore that peace as best we possibly can.

In truth, peace hardly seems a strong enough word to describe all of this. So I suggest we use a different word for a while, and that word is 'shalom', the word for peace in the Hebrew of the Old Testament. It is a wonderfully rich word. Understanding shalom is our next task.

3 December

Shalom in the here and now

LEVITICUS 26:3–6

> If you follow my statutes and keep my commandments and observe them faithfully, I will give you your rains in their season, and the land shall yield its produce, and the trees of the field shall yield their fruit. Your threshing shall overtake the vintage, and the vintage shall overtake the sowing; you shall eat your bread to the full, and live securely in your land. And I will grant peace [shalom] in the land, and you shall lie down, and no one shall make you afraid; I will remove dangerous animals from the land, and no sword shall go through your land.

What does the word 'peace' conjure up for you? The mid-morning tea break? A day to yourself? Or just one of those snatched moments when you're with friends or family and you realise 'this is good, really good'? These are helpful ways into understanding what peace is about, because they address issues of well-being. Peace is the experience of contentment, of knowing that things are in good shape and harmony. Peace is being well. Peace is wholeness. Of course, peace is also much bigger than this and must include both a meaningful relationship with God and a desire that others also share in the experience of peace. But let's not rush to that place yet, as there is a danger we could overlook something important, something easily missed.

This passage in Leviticus takes us back to the years when God's people escaped from captivity in Egypt, followed by years of wandering and a desire for a place to settle, somewhere they could be at peace, where they could lay their heads, bring up their children, grow food, be safe and worship God. Was this too much to ask for?

Evidently not, for in verse 6 God promises all of this and we begin to see the multifaceted nature of God's shalom. It entails rain at the due time, crops from the land and fruit on the trees (v. 4). Moreover, there will be a surplus (v. 5) thus insulating them from the vagaries of crop failure. And there will be security and the promise that they can sleep easy at night because 'no one shall make you afraid'. Even the wild animals will be removed from the land and they will not fear invading armies (v. 6). Shalom was an intensely practical, physical notion.

This longing for the basics of life is still part of human life today. I think of the people in the city of Flint in Michigan, USA, whose water source was changed in 2014 and subsequently they discovered that the level of lead in the new source far exceeded safe levels. The whole community was afraid of the consequences. They were certainly not at peace. Nor is a family I know whose two children cannot find work as there are no jobs in their local area – imagine how that robs them of peace! In other parts of the world, the experience of living under a corrupt regime where the rule of law is denied is normal but deeply disturbing, while large swathes of the Middle East have been overshadowed by war and the impact of Islamic fundamentalists. In the 21st century, lack of food, shelter, water and simple medication still blights the lives of millions, who also simply crave peace.

The word 'shalom' addresses all of these situations and is without doubt one of the richest words in scripture. God promises 'peace in the land' and not just peace in our hearts. Shalom embraces every facet of life.

This harmony is clearly grounded in the covenant relationship between God and his people. Verse 3 says, 'If you follow my statutes and keep my commandments and observe them faithfully.' There is an expectation that the shalom of God is part of a living relationship with him. This must not be twisted into saying that God will offer peace but first he demands something in exchange. That isn't the sense here. What God is saying is that obedience, as the fruit of a living relationship, simply creates the conditions for shalom to flourish, rather than shalom being offered as a reward for good behaviour or withheld as a punishment for disobedience.

Shalom, then, as mentioned in yesterday's reading, is an embodied, practical experience. A simple example can illustrate. I don't know when you last consumed palm oil. You probably can't remember, but the answer may well be today, because you'll find it in snack foods, ice cream, biscuits, chocolate, cereals and so on. The demand for palm oil is huge, because it's used today to replace harmful trans fat, which used to be present in much of our food. So that's good for us. On the other side of the world, however, in Asia, Africa and Latin America, our growing need for palm oil is the leading cause of deforestation. The loss of those habitats affects countless families and animals, and entails huge releases of carbon, which in turn drives climate change. As a result of this and actions like it, millions are being affected by floods and cyclones, droughts and heatwaves, as our global climate changes, and that's before we reckon with the effect on millions of people who live in the forest or off its produce.

Our actions and choices affect the lives of others, and God's word encourages us to love our neighbours as ourselves. The decisions we can make – to eat differently, to walk more, to fly less, and a thousand other choices – would be in line with God's encouragement to think of others before self. As a result, together we might experience more of God's shalom by thinking compassionately about our world neighbours. In this way, we also see that shalom has to be for everyone, or it won't be shalom. How can I be at peace if my neighbour's life is broken? Shalom is for everyone or it's for no one.

We're ready now for the next leap we have to make, which is to connect our understanding of shalom not just with our relationship with God, not just with making the world a better place, but as a step towards the biggest vision of all, a renewed heaven and a renewed earth. And tantalisingly, we get our first glimpse of how the Christmas story fits in.

4 December

Shalom in the times to come

ISAIAH 11:1-3, 6-9

A shoot shall come out from the stock of Jesse,
   and a branch shall grow out of his roots.
The spirit of the Lord shall rest on him,
   the spirit of wisdom and understanding,
   the spirit of counsel and might,
   the spirit of knowledge and the fear of the Lord.
His delight shall be in the fear of the Lord...
The wolf shall live with the lamb,
   the leopard shall lie down with the kid,
the calf and the lion and the fatling together,
   and a little child shall lead them.
The cow and the bear shall graze,
   their young shall lie down together;
   and the lion shall eat straw like the ox.
The nursing child shall play over the hole of the asp,
   and the weaned child shall put its hand on the adder's den.
They will not hurt or destroy
   on all my holy mountain;
for the earth will be full of the knowledge of the Lord
   as the waters cover the sea.

Isaiah 11 is one of the great passages foretelling the arrival of the Messiah. In verse 1 we read of Jesse, the father of David, Israel's revered king. One who is the shoot of Jesse (upon whom the Spirit of the Lord will rest) implies a future descendant in the royal line. In his genealogy, Matthew links Jesus to David, David to Jesse and Jesse to *Abraham* (see Matthew 1:1-17) as a scene setter to his account of the nativity. In doing so the gospel writer makes clear that Jesus is the fulfilment of God's promise to Abraham to call a people to himself (see Genesis 12:1–3).

Luke's gospel also has a genealogy (3:23–38), which links Jesus to David, David to Jesse and Jesse back to *Adam*, highlighting that the Messiah will reverse all that has been lost following the fall.

So far, so wonderful! But the exciting new insight in verses 6–9 above seems to reach beyond what we have encountered so far. Yes, peace is available to all who are part of the family of faith; yes, that peace is something that has practical consequences for everyone today, and for the mission of the church. But these verses seem to anticipate a day when all that we think of as normal will be changed. Who can envisage a day when a wolf and a lamb will cuddle up together? Can you imagine a day when a lion and a calf will be led out for a stroll by a child? A baby not yet weaned playing with a snake? What is all this about?

What seems to be happening is that all the taken-for-granted hostility, animosity and violence of the world has been replaced by the experience of harmony. There is a 'joy unspeakable' here in these images, and an echo of Eden is clearly intended as we recall the dominion given to humankind in Genesis 1:26–28. These verses in Isaiah are forward-looking of course, a consequence of the emergence from the line of David of the Messiah, confirmed by John's visionary account of Jesus underlining that he is the root and descendant of David (Revelation 22:16).

Fast forward from Isaiah to that Bethlehem night and we can see each of these facets unfolding. The God who was *presencing* himself among us was coming not only to embody the Abrahamic family of faith and extend it to the whole world (Galatians 3:14) and not only to reverse the sin of Adam (Romans 5:12, 18), but also as a sign that one day the experience of God's creation glimpsed in Eden would be renewed for eternity (Revelation 21:5).

These things have consequences for how we live and how we express the task of the church as it participates in the mission of God.

- We will declare the name of Jesus as the forgiver of our sinful rebellion – our *evangelism* ministry.
- We will express compassion at all times among the world's poor and downtrodden, the forgotten and the neglected, the used and the abused, and we will invite them into the family of faith – our *mercy* ministries.
- And we will also hold before us, and before a broken world, the sure and certain hope of a renewed creation when all things will find their fulfilment in Christ – our *prophetic* task.

Every element of this narrative – every man, woman and child who ever lived; every plant and animal; every atom in existence – came into being through Jesus (John 1:3) and everything has been reconciled in Jesus (Colossians 1:20) and one day that reconciliation will be actualised in a new earth and a new heaven (Revelation 21:1). This is the broad sweep of scripture, and Jesus clearly is at its heart.

If our quest is for the peace that 'surpasses all understanding' (Philippians 4:7), it cannot be found outside of Jesus. We are a Jesus people, or we have nothing to offer a hurting world. But for all of this to come about, Jesus needed to come into the experience of those he had created. The Christmas story is the end of the beginning of God's story, and the beginning of its end.

5 December

Shalom and the image of God

JOHN 1:1–2; GENESIS 1:27

> In the beginning was the Word, and the Word was with God, and the Word was God. He was in the beginning with God...
>
> So God created humankind in his image, in the image of God he created them; male and female he created them.

I am not the greatest reader of instructions! Having arrived home with my flat-pack furniture, I am more likely to get going on the project than I am to patiently lay out the parts, count them each according to their grouping, and read the leaflet provided before making a start. Not unsurprisingly, there have been times when I have had to start again as I puzzle over a problem that might have been avoided if I'd been a little wiser and gone back to start at square one.

So far, we have explored the nature of peace, or shalom, and how it might be expressed in our lives, in the lives of others and, in time, in the whole of creation. But such shalom is not just God's best idea for our human flourishing. Shalom reflects something in the very being of God, and we glimpse that in the description of creation back at the beginning of the Bible – back at square one.

The French theologian Henri Blocher, in his wonderful commentary on Genesis, addresses the importance of the study of this foundational book in the Bible, and writes that 'frequently, the *beginning* unlocks the *principle*, the *constitution* reveals the *nature*. The human race quite rightly feels it cannot find its bearings for life today without having light shed on its origins.'[1]

This, I believe, is why our quest for peace today must begin with the originator of that peace. There are two obvious places to begin: the book of Genesis and the gospel of John, both of which open with the evocative words, 'In the beginning'.

In John 1:1–2 we get an early allusion to the community within the Trinity when John says, 'In the beginning was the Word, and the Word was with God, and the Word was God. He was in the beginning with God.' If we are looking for signs that the presence of God with us is intrinsic to an experience of peace, we see that even within the Godhead there is community and togetherness. God knows nothing of separation from God, and nor should we.

In Genesis 1:26–27 we read, 'Then God said, "Let us make humankind in our image, according to our likeness"… So God created humankind in his image, in the image of God he created them; male and female he created them.' Given that God rejoiced in the creation of humankind in his image, calling it 'very good' (Genesis 1:31), and given that these verses precede the fall, we must conclude that at this time God's shalom was most perfectly present.

But what are we to make of the phrase 'in our image, according to our likeness'? What is it about being in the image of God that means creation is at peace? It is an understatement to say this is a much-debated mystery.

Over the centuries some have interpreted the image of God in a *substantive* sense; that is, there is something in the substance of what we are that is a reflection of God. The focus has been on our ability to think, to reason, to reflect. Many theologians have been attracted to this view – hardly surprising when your job is to think on God! Certainly our unique desire and ability to search for meaning sets us apart from all other species.

Others have understood the image of God in a *functional* sense, arguing that just as God has dominion over all the universe, so we read that humankind is to have dominion over the earth. Significantly, the specific reference to 'God created humankind in his image' (Genesis 1:27) is both preceded by a statement of intent to give them dominion (v. 26) and followed by a declaration that God gave them that dominion (v. 28).

Yet another school of thought argues for the image of God to be understood in a *relational* sense. For example, Karl Barth, the great 20th-century theologian, argued that the image consists of the parallel between humankind in its maleness and femaleness reflecting the internal 'face-to-face' communion of Father, Son and Holy Spirit within God.

However the image of God is to be understood, humankind was at peace, living in the experience of shalom. Here, therefore, are three areas to ponder.

If the image of God is *substantive*, to do with our capacity to reason, to think and contemplate, to search for meaning beyond ourselves, maybe this is why we experience anxiety and fear so much, because we are out of relationship with our creator, searching for that which is beyond our human reach. Peace can be restored, at least in part, when that connection with God is restored, the sin that separates is forgiven and guilt is lifted. Part of the mission of the church will be to point people back to God, so that healing can be achieved.

If the image of God relates to the *function* of being given dominion over the earth, might this not explain how our sinfulness has led us to the point where we run the risk of destroying the very earth gifted to us? Dominion has become exploitative, with us taking to ourselves what we want (and more than we need) at the cost of those who cannot have what they need. Dominion was never intended to be an exercise in exploitation, yet we have allowed it to become so. There is a dis-ease in many of us brought about by our desire to have more things, or for companies to make more profits, while ignoring the ravaging effect this has on God's creation and those who are among the have-nots. Part of the mission of the church must be to remind us of our responsibility to be good stewards of that which God has entrusted to us.

If the image of God is to do with our *relational* capacity, might that not explain why we are so often ill at ease with others, alienated, lonely or disconnected? The prevalence of racism, xenophobia and gender-based violence in multiple forms (including pornography, sexism, domestic violence and rape as a tool of war) illustrates how our ability to relate to 'the other' is severely damaged. Part of the mission of the church must be to help people out of destructive behaviours and into a sense of our shared humanity, sisters and brothers created together in the image of God.

There isn't space here to reconcile these differing views, or adjudicate between them. But they make the point that, just as peace rests on us knowing the presence of God, knowing the presence of God demands of us a journey back to that place where the image of God is restored and expressed in our lives. Peace is a gift but it is also something we must work at.

What these different insights have in common is that peace is far more than something for us as individuals. It has implications for the whole of humanity, and indeed the cosmos. As Christmas approaches, we remind ourselves that what is about to take place has personal, global and cosmic significance.

6 December

Shalom and the purposes of heaven

LUKE 2:8–14

> In that region there were shepherds living in the fields, keeping watch over their flock by night. Then an angel of the Lord stood before them, and the glory of the Lord shone around them, and they were terrified. But the angel said to them, 'Do not be afraid; for see – I am bringing you good news of great joy for all the people: to you is born this day in the city of David a Saviour, who is the Messiah, the Lord. This will be a sign for you: you will find a child wrapped in bands of cloth and lying in a manger. And suddenly there was with the angel a multitude of the heavenly host, praising God and saying, 'Glory to God in the highest heaven, and on earth peace among those whom he favours!'

On 14 February 1990, the spacecraft *Voyager*, launched 13 years earlier, took a photograph of Earth from a distance of 3.7 billion miles. The photograph became famous as 'The Pale Blue Dot', a reminder that this vast and mind-blowingly beautiful world we live in is just, in the words of the astronomer Carl Sagan, 'a mote of dust, suspended in a sunbeam'.

One of our challenges as human beings is that we often struggle to hold together seemingly conflicting realities. There is the absolute truth of our significance within God's creation, yet also the humbling truth of our physical insignificance within it. There is something undeniable in our grandeur and yet also in our pettiness. We are creators of awesome beauty but also the authors of indescribable horrors. We are capable of exhibiting mastery over the universe, yet incapable of mastery over our own hearts and minds.

It is within these tensions that we live and enjoy fleeting moments of peace, yet always mindful of the tendency for that peace to be shattered by the cruel intrusions of a harsher reality. In these places we can be tempted to find a quiet uninterruptible corner where we can hide and enjoy our own secret undisturbed peace. But we can only do that at the cost of shutting out the disturbing voices of others who also desire their share of that same peace; they require my spiritual and ethical engagement in the process of helping them realise that peace. We may be just a single point of life on that pale blue dot, but we have been created in such a way that in our best moments we can understand and embrace our wider responsibilities within it.

To achieve this, we must inhabit two ends of a spectrum. We live in one place where peace is a matter for my soul, for my well-being, for my 'here and now'. This peace, as we have already seen, is intrinsically bound up in my relationship with the God who created me in Christ Jesus. But peace is not just my personal thing; it is not even just for my family or my community. It is for the world in which we live, and in our most expansive moments our minds race beyond the pale blue dot and we can even consider how the cosmos itself may find a new peace.

If you have come to this season of your life seeking peace, I hope and pray this book, in some small way, helps you to find it or retain it or maybe develop it. But if our understanding of peace remains centred on ourselves and our own needs, we will have failed. The peace of God that surpasses all understanding, everyone's understanding, is something that encompasses the whole of creation, every atom and molecule, every man and woman, every animal and plant, every mountain and river, every pale blue dot and every other dot of whatever colour flung into the far reaches of space. Peace is the whole of creation in harmony with its creator.

We find echoes of this in scripture. The echoes may be faint, because the horizons of the Old and New Testament writers were more limited than ours. But the echoes are there, especially on those occasions or in the places when the closeness of heaven and earth becomes what the Celtic Christians called 'thin places'.

One such place was a Judean hillside on the night the angels appeared. A seemingly familiar scene, because of the countless nativity plays we have seen with youngsters adorned in dressing gowns, tea towels and gossamer wings. Off to the side are the lucky two who have been chosen to play Mary and Joseph, and the others whose role as sheep and goats will still leave mums, dads and grandparents dewy-eyed!

But on the night itself, that first night, this was a thin place. First one angel came and spoke, and the shepherds were terrified, as you'd expect. 'Do not be afraid' was part of the liturgy, as it had been when Mary had an angel appear to her. Then, after the first angel came a throng of angels, a multitude of the heavenly host. Wherever heaven is and whatever heaven is like, a glimpse of its angelic ambassadors is surely enough to scare us witless! But their witness was unmistakable: 'Glory to God in the highest heaven, and on earth peace among those whom he favours!' (v. 14).

How quick we can be to point out the innocence of the old triple-decker universe (heaven above, hell below and earth in between), but we have no better idea ourselves. All we know is that the angels came to announce that in heaven it is God's glory that is predominant, while here in this thin place, here in this point in human history, we have come to announce the in-breaking of peace. Just as it was God's purpose in the beginning to create, so now it is God's purpose to redeem.

The angels, heaven's ambassadors, came with the good news that the people had long cried for. Life was hard. Society was corrupt, even at the hands of their own people, some of whom had become collaborators – tax collectors. Harvests were erratic, violence was frequent, life expectancy was short and the Roman occupation was brutal. The angels had not come for a peace party.

But they had come to announce that after generations of waiting for the Messiah of Israel, the promise was about to be fulfilled. Within a few miles of this hillside a child was born in Bethlehem. The birth of the child heralded the promise of peace and marked a critical juncture in God's redemption plan. The peace of God and the presence of God are once again inextricably linked.

7 December

Shalom and good order

GENESIS 1:28–31

> God blessed them, and God said to them, 'Be fruitful and
> multiply, and fill the earth and subdue it; and have dominion
> over the fish of the sea and over the birds of the air and over
> every living thing that moves upon the earth.' God said, 'See,
> I have given you every plant yielding seed that is upon the
> face of all the earth, and every tree with seed in its fruit; you
> shall have them for food. And to every beast of the earth,
> and to every bird of the air, and to everything that creeps on
> the earth, everything that has the breath of life, I have given
> every green plant for food.' And it was so. God saw everything
> that he had made, and indeed, it was very good.

God blessed them. And with these simple words from our text above,
we see what that blessing looked like. The seas, the skies and the
land were teeming with life. There was food in plentiful supply, and
there is no mention of dangers from pestilence, wild animals and
the like. Here we see creation ordered in a way that was designed to
enable life to flourish in harmony.

The narrative of Genesis 1 and 2 is one of careful, creative structuring
of the most unbelievable complexity. The poetic structure of the text
alone betrays something of that order in ways that are often missed.
There is a beautiful symmetry in the six days of creation, for instance
where days one to three parallel days four to six. Days one and four
involve the creation of light and lights. Day two entails the separation
of the seas from the sky and day four sees the emergence of creatures
of the sea and the birds in the sky. Day three sees the creation of the
land and its vegetation, while day six sees the creation upon that

land of animal life and, the pinnacle of creation, humankind. This is divine poetry at its best, and it conveys truth and beauty of the highest order. It does not tell us the physics and chemistry of the creative process, but it clearly reveals its author, and the motivations and hopes inherent in that process.

The important point here is that God is seen as a God of order. The creation process has a rhythmic repetition – day building on day, each sparked by the creative word 'And God said', and each ending with what can almost humorously be seen as God standing back at the close of a busy day, reflecting on his work and sighing, 'that's good!'

Indeed, if we but have eyes to see it, the whole of creation belies an extraordinary sense of order. From the beauty of everyday flower petals to the intricate symmetry of a snowflake. From the tracks of the planets around stars to the motion of atoms moving within molecules. Complex mathematics betray an almost incomprehensible structuring within the universe that we would be hard-pressed to see as the result of chance. Creation is ordered, and that ordering reflects the nature of God himself. Order does not mean repetition or lack of creativity – anyone who has seen a kitten or a toddler at play can hardly accuse God of being unimaginative! Rather, order is a corollary of security, of trust in people and things and the future. Order, if we only recognised it, is what makes our lives both bearable and enjoyable.

In the mission work I have been involved in for many years, in many different countries, we have often had people working in hostile environments. Some have lived in war zones, where the threat to their safety was from bombs falling from the sky or a suicide bomber on the bus. I have travelled to Afghanistan during the Taliban years and to North Korea under the current regime and, frankly, felt no obvious danger, but consistently the greatest threat to our personnel has been in places where law and order broke down, chaos ensued, and crowds rampaged through the streets. These are the times of greatest risk, when people do the most unimaginable things. We have evacuated more people in these circumstances than in more stable, even if hostile, situations.

Order is a good thing, without question, and order is discernible in the creation story and in the relationship that Adam and Eve had with God. There is an unmistakable sense of God desiring what was best for them. He creates one for the other in a beautiful act of mutuality, creates a garden idyll for them to thrive and reproduce in and to have dominion over, and he gives them the privilege of naming the different species. I wonder if we have lost sight of the goodness of what it means to have dominion over something – a responsibility, yes, but also a great privilege. God creates Adam and Eve in his own image, talks with them, takes delight in them and, what is truly awesome, is pictured as walking in the garden and calling them out by name. Here we see something of the relationship God wants with all those he has created.

My own life today has a reasonable sense of order that is pleasant and good. I have a secure home, a regular income, good health, access to medical care, a steady food supply, clean water and money in the bank. Moreover, I have my faith and, because of that, a clear sense of who I am, of what my life is about and of my destiny. Yes, all is reasonably well in my part of the garden! But for millions less fortunate than I am, this multitude of provisions – from food to faith, from medicine to money – would be a foretaste of heaven itself. The things I take for granted as blessings from a bountiful God are out of reach for so many in today's world. The church's mission, therefore, is always to find ways to make these kingdom provisions available to people today. Of course, even these things, as good as they are, pale in comparison to the riches of God's renewed heaven and earth, but to those without hope or meaning in their lives, the broken, the thirsty and the homeless, they are the first fruits of God's kingdom.

There is order within creation, order also in the relationship with Adam and Eve, and order too in the grand sweep of God's salvation story in scripture. We will explore various elements of this as we go through these studies, but the way God chose to unfold his redemptive plan was no accident. It involved the calling of Abram, the pledge of a land to him, and the evident protection of God over his family in successive generations. Later generations would be released from captivity not once but twice, in Egypt and Babylon. The prophetic seeds of the coming of a Saviour were sown by the prophets. Then Mary was chosen, along with Joseph, and the earthly life of our Lord was seen through to its dramatic conclusion on the cross, at the resurrection tomb, and through the related events of the ascension and Pentecost. This story is still unfolding today, and a time is set in the heart of God when Christ will return and all of history finds its fullness in him.

This redemption drama is for everyone, without exception, but maybe those with most to gain will identify with it more readily. Perhaps that's why the Christmas story was set in the context of poverty, danger, occupation by enemy forces and the threat to life. Perhaps that's why the Christian faith thrives today largely outside the more ordered, secure western world.

8 December

Shalom and the entry of chaos

Read GENESIS 3:8–13

> **But the Lord God called to the man, and said to him, 'Where are you?' He said, 'I heard the sound of you in the garden, and I was afraid, because I was naked; and I hid myself.' He said, 'Who told you that you were naked? Have you eaten from the tree of which I commanded you not to eat?'**
>
> vv. 9–11

The presence of God amid his perfect creation was epitomised in the experience of Eden. Here was peace as God intended, the shalom of which the Bible speaks. Here is a completeness that expressed the very heart of God for those he brought into being and loved. Here was a perfection that reminds us of the distinction between the creation of the cosmos, which was deemed *good*, and the creation of humankind, which was deemed *very good*. In these early chapters of Genesis we glimpse in multiple ways the ease and the normality of the relationship between God and Adam and Eve. God instructs Adam on what is to be eaten in the garden (Genesis 2:16–17), and so we see the beginnings of an interactive relationship between God and those he created. When that interaction is open, untainted by sin and characterised by loving obedience, we surely see peace, the universe as it was meant to be.

We see it also in the nakedness of Adam and Eve before God, where we read that, though naked, they felt no shame (Genesis 2:25). In today's sexualised world it can be difficult to understand the significance of this verse, and our focus can be drawn initially to their nudity. However, the focus should be on the absence of shame, which is how people at the time, who saw nakedness as evidence of destitution or disgrace, would have understood it. Here their nakedness speaks of complete openness, the lack of necessity to conceal anything from themselves or from God. It speaks of humanity's ability to know and be known in our entirety. It speaks of a nature that sees no need to hide, where there is no sense of anxiety. Here too we see peace.

But suddenly, and horrifically if you consider all that flowed over the aeons to come from humankind's inability to live according to God's word, everything changes. You may remember the Joni Mitchell classic 'Big Yellow Taxi', with the reminder that we don't know what we've got until it's gone. Here, too, we gain an understanding of peace even in the very act of that peace disappearing. In Genesis 3:1 we eavesdrop on a conversation where Eve is being asked by the serpent, 'Did God really say that?' and it's hard not to sense that this conversation is an unhealthy one. In the act of disobeying God the first thing that changes is that the eyes of both of them are opened, and they realise they are naked (Genesis 3:7). Shalom is evaporating like the morning mist, and yet we gain one more painful insight into what is happening as we are told that 'they heard the sound of the Lord God walking in the garden at the time of the evening breeze, and the man and his wife hid themselves from the presence of the Lord God among the trees of the garden' (v. 8).

The easy communion with God and with themselves is lost. The achingly beautiful openness they shared is replaced by shame, lack of disclosure, the building of barriers, the blaming of the other and the erosion of trust. Here we glimpse what peace is like even as we see it disappear from before our eyes. And as that peace evaporates, the yawning chasm opens between the creator and his creation. Paradise is truly lost and with it the peace that surpasses all understanding.

Now we begin to see what a chaotic world looks like. The earth becomes a place of toil, yielding its fruits begrudgingly. Cain murders Abel, the whole generation of Noah's day are wiped out by a flood,

Abram and Sara fail to trust in God's promise, God's people are enslaved in Egypt and eventually 'all the people did what was right in their own eyes' (Judges 21:25). And so I could continue to the present day.

Yesterday, I said that my own experience of life has been reasonably well ordered, thank you very much! But I hinted that this was a judgement made upon my scales, not God's. For the truth is that everything we touch turns to ruin. The best of intentions, the best of relationships, the best of achievements and the best of our kindnesses fall short of the glory of God. They fall short by a million miles. They fall so far short that we cannot even see what a life of shalom with God can be like. How could we? All has been lost.

Or has it? Almost at the point when humanly speaking our grief should cause us to yield to the darkness, there is a tiny glimmer of light. When we rightly think that everything is lost, we see something in the Christmas story that offers us a slim hope that what is broken can be made whole again. It is simply this – the mystery that Mary, the mother of Jesus, created in the image of God, is capable of bearing the life of Jesus. Think not of Jesus the unborn child or newborn infant. Think of Jesus through whom all that has been made was made; who made the whole of creation out of nothing; who, in what is almost a throwaway line, is described as the one who 'also made the stars' (Genesis 1:16, NIV). Think of Jesus who was before time began and will be when time is finished, and of whom the writer to the Hebrews says is 'the reflection of God's glory and the exact imprint of God's very being' (Hebrews 1:3).

This embryonic, incarnate Jesus is breathed into the womb of Mary by the Holy Spirit of God. The cosmos is hushed. There is yet a way for this peace to be restored, but at an unimaginable cost!

9 December

Shalom and the cross of Christ

COLOSSIANS 1:15–20

> He is the image of the invisible God, the firstborn of all creation; for in him all things in heaven and on earth were created, things visible and invisible, whether thrones or dominions or rulers or powers – all things have been created through him and for him. He himself is before all things, and in him all things hold together. He is the head of the body, the church; he is the beginning, the firstborn from the dead, so that he might come to have first place in everything. For in him all the fullness of God was pleased to dwell, and through him God was pleased to reconcile to himself all things, whether on earth or in heaven, by making peace through the blood of his cross.

You may have noticed by now that there is both a subjective and an objective dimension to this thing we have called peace. Subjectively, it can be how we feel or don't feel. The events of everyday life produce circumstances whereby we feel we have or feel we lack the peace we desire. Objectively, the Bible also speaks of peace in a different way. In today's passage, there is no reference to how we feel; rather there is a bold statement that through Christ God made peace with 'all things... through the blood of his cross' (v. 20). We need to understand what is being said here.

This passage is one of the high peaks of scripture. It addresses in magisterial terms the greatness and uniqueness of Christ. With echoes of other biblical texts, we are told that Christ is the image of the invisible God (v. 15 and Hebrew 1:3), that everything was created by him and for him (v. 16 and John 1:3), that he was before time began (v. 18 and John 17:5), that he sustains all things (v. 17 and Hebrews 1:3) and that he has first place in everything (v. 18 and 1 Corinthians 8:6). What is unmistakable and undeniable is the absolute exaltation of Jesus. He is high and lifted up, worthy of all honour and praise.

But verse 20 reminds us that Jesus came in the flesh for a purpose, and the purpose was not simply to make us feel better – at least not in the direct sense we might mean. For example, if the passage said all the above about Jesus but then closed by saying that he lived a long and holy life and died in old age in his home in Nazareth, it would offer me some solace that he knew what it meant to live our kind of life and knew the kind of problems that come to us, but apart from added inspiration, nothing has really changed.

What did change is alluded to in verse 20: God our Father, through Jesus his Son, our Saviour, reconciled 'all things… by making peace through the blood of his cross'. Take your minds back to the Passover night we discussed on 2 December, and Jesus' assertion that he had to leave his disciples (John 16:6–7). The compulsion to leave was not a desire to part company from them, but 'he set his face to go to Jerusalem' (Luke 9:51) because the hour had come 'for the Son of Man to be glorified' (John 12:23). Here then is the heart of what it means to engage with the peace that surpasses all understanding. It is an objective peace – something that has been made possible solely by the intervention of God. Something was changed that has altered the relationship between God and humankind.

Some years ago, I attended a circus. While the lions and tigers were impressive, the clowns funny and the trapeze artists unbelievably brave, it was a plate-spinning act that I remember best. It was funny and clever and as engaging as any other performance that day. When the plates were spinning level, all was well, but the moment they started to wobble, the audience screamed and gesticulated to tell the spinner where to go next.

That image of the plate wobbling is one of my abiding images of what the Bible calls sin. The wobble may be small, or it may be catastrophic, but you can tell immediately that it's not on the level. The only thing that can correct the situation is the intervention of the plate spinner to bring things back to right.

Now there is a flaw in most illustrations, so don't stretch this beyond its limit. The thing is, the whole of creation has wobbled since the intrusion of sin. Today we still struggle with understanding what that means, but we look around and we sure don't have to struggle to understand the reality of it. Even on our good days, our purest motivations, our kindest deeds are at best but fleeting moments, at worst tainted by disordered motivation.

We have seen that from the outset God's wonderful creation fell into a state of rebellion by the defiance of those he created and to whom he gave free will. Somewhere and somehow, in the unseen order of things that embraces our human lives, the lives of animals and even the physical universe itself, life became out of sync with God.

Imagine the cumulative effect of these countless wobbles. Lives hurting, broken and stunted; violence and rebellion; abuse and disuse; relationships twisted; sickness and pain; accidents and tragedy; depression and self-loathing; hatred and fighting; battles and wars; death and dying. Taken together they comprise an insurmountable barrier between God and ourselves. They rob us of any opportunity to enjoy the presence of God.

But the news is good, not bad, because God has acted and in Christ he has made peace by his death on the cross. You see, every wobbling plate, left alone, will crash to the floor and smash into pieces. That is the death that is the natural consequence of our disordered lives. Not all is bad, of course not, but objectively we are separated from God, who is infinitely holy. It is because of this that Jesus enters our human experience to take on to himself all that is laid upon us.

Romans 5:12–21 expresses this well, and this is where our gospel has huge coherence. Jesus was sinless and so did not deserve to die. That cannot be said of anyone else. But as the innocent one, he died on our behalf, and in that act of dying he took the sin of the world into himself and took them down into death. We cannot plumb the depths of understanding required to make sense of how that 'death of death' took place, but we do know that if the cross and resurrection of Jesus means anything, it will be the diametric opposite of the sum total of human wretchedness that sits on the other side of the scales.

Christ's resurrection was the evidence that death itself had been destroyed and peace was now, at last, possible. One day it will be wholly realised, but for now a foretaste is possible. In Romans 5:1 we read, 'Therefore, since we are justified by faith, we have peace with God through our Lord Jesus Christ', and in John 10:10 we read the words of Jesus, 'I came that they may have life, and have it abundantly.'

Peace is possible now, in this life, through a living faith relationship with God. And over the coming days I want us to see how God's people have been able to search out that peace for themselves, even in the midst of many trials.

Part II

Saints in search of peace

10 December

Joseph: peace in the face of betrayal

Read GENESIS 50:15–21

> But Joseph said to them, 'Do not be afraid! Am I in the place of God? Even though you intended to do harm to me, God intended it for good, in order to preserve a numerous people, as he is doing today.'
> vv. 19–20

I grew up as one of four brothers and have the bruises to show for it, or rather the missing teeth! Life was fun, and there was lots of rough and tumble, but we survived our childhood years and remain good friends today. Joseph's experience was different. He was the youngest, his father's favourite (Genesis 37:3), and as a result was probably a bit cocky, in need of being brought down a peg or two. Matters became worse when Joseph told his brothers about a dream he had in which he saw them bowing down before him (Genesis 37:7). In another dream, Joseph said the sun, moon and stars bowed before him, something that even irked his fawning father (Genesis 37:10). As a result, his brothers threw him in a well, then sold him to passing traders going to Egypt and told Jacob, their father, a lie – that Joseph had been killed.

Joseph's life took many twists and turns, some for the better, others for worse. And many years later when the brothers found themselves in front of him and begged for forgiveness, he was gracious and uttered the well-known words: 'Even though you intended to do harm to me, God intended it for good' (Genesis 50:20). Like a play in the theatre, all's well that ends well.

Except life isn't like that. For years Joseph was separated from his family, hated by his brothers, living among strangers, wrongly accused of rape by his employer's wife and thrown into prison. Yes, he did well in Egypt, but life was hard at times and all the while he lived with the pain of estrangement from those with whom the bonds of family love should have been paramount. He must have longed to see his homeland again and his father, maybe even his brothers too. But he lived without these things and yet served God faithfully over the years. When his brothers were eventually before him, but before they recognised him, he was unable to contain himself any longer, broke down in tears and revealed to his brothers that he was Joseph, the one they had sold into slavery (Genesis 45:1). The uncontrolled release of those tears reveal more than words can tell that he had bottled up his emotions over the years to a degree we cannot overestimate.

Peace can be ours, as we have seen, in all kinds of circumstances, but sometimes it needs to be lived in spite of those circumstances and not simply because the badness is removed. There will be times when we too hold back the tears, suppressing our true emotions and conveying to the outside world that all is well. It may be in the face of those who have done harm to us, like Joseph's brothers. But it may also be in the face of those we love distancing themselves from us, or taking a path we believe not to be right for them. Parents sometimes have to let go and pray that God will take care of those they can no longer guide or influence as once they could.

The question, however, is how we find peace in these circumstances. Let me suggest four ways that may be of help.

First, we can pray for those we love and from whom we may have become estranged. Yes, it can be hard to do this if those concerned have been hurtful, unthinking or downright selfish. But praying for them will not be hard if we still long for there to be reconciliation. There will still be a love there that laments what has happened and longs to find a better way. Prayers may not be answered the way we want, but the very act of praying, taking their name into the presence of God, can soften even the hardest of hearts. The love that Joseph showed towards his brothers in the later chapters of Genesis surely suggests that he had nurtured a love for his family all through the years, and likely he will have prayed for them.

Second, go on living. Your life does not wholly depend on your relationship with another. Yes, it will be different and it may even be painful, but it doesn't stop. Joseph continued to use his skills and insights to bring blessing to those he served and those over whom he had power. The years pass quickly and too much time living with regrets can rob us of the privilege of being available in the service of God.

Third, insofar as you can, love those who have hurt you. It serves our own purposes to portray others always as the baddies, as those who have no redeeming features, and ourselves as the saints! In my experience, even if the blame lies wholly on one side, little is gained by obscuring anything that is good in the other. The beginning of reconciliation and forgiveness is a recognition that there is goodness even in those we are angry with.

Fourth, believe in the overarching purposes of God. I don't mean by that to imply that wrongdoing is sanctioned by God for the attainment of some higher purpose. God was not the author of the horrendous deeds of Joseph's brothers. But rather it is a way of saying that even when bad things happen, God can *purpose* that event to realise some good. He didn't initiate it, but he can redeem it.

11 December

Ruth: peace when faced with difficult decisions

Read RUTH 1:1–17

> Then they wept aloud again. Orpah kissed her mother-in-law, but Ruth clung to her. So she said, 'See, your sister-in-law has gone back to her people and to her gods; return after your sister-in-law.' But Ruth said, 'Do not press me to leave you or to turn back from following you! Where you go, I will go; where you lodge, I will lodge; your people shall be my people, and your God my God. Where you die, I will die – there will I be buried. May the Lord do thus and so to me, and more as well, if even death parts me from you!'
>
> vv. 14–17

Over the years I have carried my share of leadership responsibility for enabling mission workers to live in lands where safety was far from guaranteed. Our missionaries have been held up at gunpoint in the street and taken to an ATM for cash, tied up with their children in their home by burglars carrying knives, had mortar attacks blow out their windows, and endured the execution of their friends at the hands of those they came to serve. I know these people well enough to know that, on the one hand, they are just ordinary faithful Christians who are focused on following God wherever he calls them to be; on the other hand, I also know them to be *extraordinary* faithful Christians who are focused on following God wherever he calls them to be!

In our own mission history, we have stories of those who took their belongings to Congo in a coffin, knowing it might be a useful thing to have with them. I've stood in graveyards in Africa, Asia and the Caribbean and reflected on the young age of those from BMS World Mission who had died in pursuit of their calling. In some of these places the church is now established, thriving even, and people's lives are transformed as a result. These pioneers are heroes, but I always remind myself and others that they are only heroes in retrospect, often long after they have died. When they were alive they faced a real choice. Do I go and take a great risk, often with my family too, or do I stay here? And having gone, do I stay, at great risk to self and family, or do I return home?

Today there are men and women, often with children, in different countries wrestling with the same issues. Like most mission workers they will be forgotten by all except family and friends in the years to come. No one will write a book about them. Most will be, in human terms, a footnote on a page in some future history. In the meantime, they hear the words of Naomi saying, 'Go home' or 'Come home', just as Ruth and Orpah did. These come from the voices of good people, sensible, well-intentioned and prayerful voices of those for whom the burden of concern is even heavier at a distance than the burden of living out the calling on the ground. These are voices laced with love and deep concern. Sometimes it is right to hear such voices, and yet sometimes it's right to respect those who say, 'No, here we stay.'

In today's world, where one false step leaves you open to being sued, one of the hardest principles we adhered to in our mission work was that, in a time of war or an outbreak of a killer disease, we would never demand that a mission worker leave their place of service. The only exception was if the national church said in a time of war that they had to go, for to stay would imperil them also. Otherwise, if our missionaries wanted to stay, we would support them in that decision.

For most of us, there are few occasions in today's world when we need to weigh our faith on the scales of life, but for many mission workers that is still a daily choice. For many it's the costly dilemma to stay in the face of separation from family, the need to care for ageing parents, or what is thought to be the best schooling option for children. For some it can be literally life and death. When people you knew, and children you knew, are killed in a land where you stand out as a foreigner and your killer could be the person walking behind you in the street, the choice is stark.

Ruth stayed with Naomi, which is not to say that to stay is always the right decision. That would be an abuse of scripture. In fact, the decision isn't best seen as one of right or wrong. Both options are crushingly heavy. Both demand godly discernment without even a whiff of censure or regret if someone decides they must come home.

Ruth's prayer quoted above suggests strongly that she had weighed her choices carefully. She loved Naomi and knew that it was right to stay. She is the hero of the story. But Orpah cried too, and she returned home. She isn't remembered as the hero of the story, but that doesn't make her a failure. She isn't 'out of God's will'. For whatever reason, she felt she had to return. For all we know it was God's will for her to return. God's will for Ruth would be fulfilled in her meeting with Boaz.

When you pray for those you know – mission workers, yes, but anyone whose calling is making a high demand of them – pray that they might make the right decision and be at peace about it. But don't assume that the right decision is always the seemingly more costly one. Recall Isaac Watts' great hymn 'When I survey the wondrous cross'. You will have sung it many times, including the lines:

Love so amazing, so divine,
Demands my soul, my life, my all.

Those words describe the commitment that all believers should bring to the decision-making process. But the commitment doesn't actually make the decision. That struggle remains, to find the will of God in the midst of complexity, and to live with the consequences.

12 December

Hannah: peace with an aching heart

Read 1 SAMUEL 1:1–8

On the day when Elkanah sacrificed, he would give portions to his wife Peninnah and to all her sons and daughters; but to Hannah he gave a double portion, because he loved her, though the Lord had closed her womb.

vv. 5–6

I'd love to meet Hannah. Though she struggled with being childless, she knew herself to be loved by her husband, Elkanah. Still, she felt vulnerable in the face of provocation from Elkanah's other wife, Peninnah. (Now isn't the time to talk about 'a traditional biblical view of marriage', but it's clearly a phrase that needs to be used cautiously!) The writer simply assumes the default theology of the day, that 'the Lord had closed her womb' (v. 6), a view that Hannah herself will have shared.

We're told that in the temple Hannah was distressed; she prayed and she wept bitterly (v. 10). The priest Eli, after an initial misunderstanding, where he thought she was drunk, blessed her and told her to go in peace. Within a short time, or so it appears, her prayer was answered and she conceived, and her son Samuel was born. Samuel was to become a great man of God.

As is the case with many Bible stories, these events are recorded because they represent key developments in the life of God's people and because they often illustrate the truth that God answers prayers; truly nothing is impossible with God. We need to know these lessons and, in the act of believing, our faith is stretched and we can aim for great things in God's name.

But before we file Hannah's story among the pages of 'great prayers God has answered', we note that there are a hundred more like Hannah whose prayers are not answered. Whether it's prayers for a spouse or a baby, a prodigal or a healing, there is no shortage of prayers uttered and apparently left unanswered. It can be tempting therefore to turn aside from Hannah, believing that she has nothing to say to those whose prayers have apparently fallen on deaf ears.

But I want to read between the lines, to go back and ask what we know of Hannah in the years before her prayer was answered. And the clue we get is in 1 Samuel 1:7, where we read, 'So it went on year by year; as often as she went up to the house of the Lord, she used to provoke her. Therefore Hannah wept and would not eat.' You see, it would be wrong to think of Hannah as one who 'simply' had a problem and God answered her prayer. In fact, God didn't answer her prayer for many years and yet, despite the unanswered prayers, she continued to seek out the presence of God. Despite the renewed humiliation delivered by Peninnah, the rival wife, she went to the temple. And despite the love of a clearly devoted husband, she wept bitterly.

As a minister there is nothing harder than to face someone struggling with a problem that is causing them deep and intense heartache and to be unable to say or do anything to help. It's our default approach to life – show me the problem and we will do all we can to fix it. And if we can't fix it, we'll show you someone who can. We live in an age of being able to fix most things, and we get frustrated and angry when we can't. We can't ultimately prevent hurricanes from devastating islands or earthquakes from flattening villages. We can't heal all cancers, and we can't prevent the deterioration that comes with Parkinson's disease or Alzheimer's. In a world where we can achieve so much we rage against the things we cannot put right. And in that rage, we can lose any semblance of peace.

Early on we saw that the peace that Jesus promised was the peace of his presence. We can cultivate that presence when we stay close to God, to God's people and to God's church, not because God is only found in our churches but because in our churches the presence of God and the loving care of God is taught and stressed again and again, and we need to hear it frequently. And hearing it, we worship as a community.

If you or someone you know is struggling with an aching heart, it's okay to weep. It's okay to say I can't even eat for a while, as Hannah did. It's okay to say we feel humiliated or powerless or dejected, because the peace of God isn't about removing these things, not always, anyway. It's even okay to grieve over these things despite having a loving parent, spouse or friend who cares for you. Being at peace isn't to deny that there are times when we want to rage against everything we hate about our circumstances. God is big enough to take our pain and our anger – even our anger directed towards him – because he too has experienced it. He entered our life; he experienced the grief of hearing that his cousin John had been beheaded, that Lazarus had died, that his disciples couldn't even stay awake and that his Father had forsaken him. He endured the cross and its inexpressible agony, as well as the experience of looking down on the face of his mother Mary as she saw him hanging there.

And if you're the carer, the lover, the one who would do anything to relieve the person in your care of their heartache, you too have to live with the fact that their anguish isn't a rejection of you but a rejection of that which is threatening to crush them.

I'd love to meet Hannah, not to ask her what it was like when she realised she was pregnant; I can almost imagine the joy of that moment. Rather, I'd like to ask her about her relationship with God in the years before. I don't believe she always *felt* peaceful – far from it. But she did know something of God's presence, and she didn't reject him because of her inability to conceive. So what *was* it she experienced? What *was* it she discovered about God in those days of aching? That's what I'd like to know.

13 December

Daniel: peace in a strange land

Read DANIEL 1:1–21

But Daniel resolved that he would not defile himself...
v. 8

A couple of years ago I preached in a large church. To be precise, it was in a large church building with a small congregation, and understandably a conversation with an elderly member lamented the passing of the years, and the much smaller numbers of attendees compared to her youth.

Now, I do not fear for the church, either in this land, where the tide seems to have gone out in my lifetime, or elsewhere in the world, where the church is often persecuted or experiencing a boom time. I do not fear, because Jesus is the head of the church. It's his church, not mine, nor yours. But we are still charged with trying to understand what is happening in these days, and seeing our current western church experience as a time of exile is, I believe, a helpful analysis. We find ourselves in a strange land, where the church is often denigrated or, worse, ignored, and where the church continues to adapt to life at the margins of society rather than at its heart.

The question is – can there be peace for us at a time like this? In a place like this? I believe there can be, but we need to play our part. While it's true that the peace of God is a gift, that is not to say that we don't have a role to play.

As we have seen so many times in these studies, the first thing to recognise is God's presence not his absence. He was right there at the beginning when his people were taken into exile – verse 2 makes it clear that God *allowed* this to happen. God is never caught off guard. He is in control even when things happen that seem contrary to his dominion and control. We see that God is present again and again, such as when he allowed Daniel to find favour in Babylon (v. 9), and of course he is with Daniel and his friends in the events of chapter 2, when Daniel is the interpreter of dreams, in the fire of chapter 3 and among the lions of chapter 6.

Today God is ever-present too: at the heart of our churches; in the ministries that thousands of churches exercise day in and day out. God is present in the preaching of his word and in the countless moments when God's grace is mediated through his people. God is alive and well today, whether the tide ebbs or flows.

But we need to play our part. Daniel knew this and could see the temptations to simply blend into the new culture around him and, to all intents and purposes, become an anonymous follower of God. In verse 5 we see them being offered a royal diet of the best food and wine and an opportunity to progress in the service of Nebuchadnezzar. Here is the seduction of the world around us, in the guise of food that Daniel knew was off limits to him if he was a devout Jew. So too for us, with the seductions of life all around us, there will be moments when we recognise that if we desire the peace of God in our lives we must refrain from the temptations before us. Today's world offers material possessions through every advert every hour of the day. Sexual temptation is never far away, whether in person or through the internet. And all too often the media exposes ways in which those with power abuse that power in pursuit of selfish ends.

Daniel resolved not to defile himself (v. 8) but said he would only eat what was right according to his religious convictions. And God rewarded him for this. But here's the complex part, because in today's changing world where the church hasn't always got things right, 'sticking to our convictions' can be a convenient cover for refusing to engage with a society that regularly throws up fresh challenges. If we had stuck with the convictions of our forefathers, the church would still condone slavery and the subjugation of women. The church has abused its power too often and damaged countless lives in appalling ways. In other words, the church cannot automatically claim the high moral ground. In the eyes of many, we have a *credibility deficit disorder* and that's where we start from. Perhaps if there is a lesson to learn in exile it's that the church abused its power when it was in control.

None of this is to dent our true convictions, that in Jesus Christ alone is the hope of the world. Exile can be a refining period in the life of the church; indeed, I believe that is happening. When it's no longer easy to be a Christian, or socially advantageous to be seen as such, there emerges a renewed strength. Here in the west we are not experiencing persecution – at worst it's 'a little local difficulty' but no more. But perhaps we can be thankful for what God is teaching us these days, even recognising the benefits of this time of pruning. Written in a different context but with real relevance to our own situation, we can recall Paul's words to the Christians in Rome:

> We also boast in our sufferings, knowing that suffering produces endurance, and endurance produces character, and character produces hope, and hope does not disappoint us, because God's love has been poured into our hearts through the Holy Spirit that has been given to us.
> ROMANS 5:3–5

It is that hope that allows us to experience peace, even when all is not as we would like it to be. Daniel devoted himself to God and made a valuable contribution to the world in which he found himself. In the same context of exile the prophet Jeremiah relayed the word of the Lord when he said to the people:

> Seek the welfare of the city where I have sent you into exile, and pray to the Lord on its behalf, for in its welfare you will find your welfare.
> JEREMIAH 29:7

Here we find no permission to wallow in inertia or self-pity, for it is God who has *sent* his people into exile. It is God who charges us to be a blessing to those around us:

> Build houses and live in them... Take wives and have sons and daughters; take wives for your sons, and give your daughters in marriage, that they may bear sons and daughters; multiply there, and do not decrease.
>
> JEREMIAH 29:5–6

Is the world as we would like it to be? Not at all. But can we experience the peace of God in this place? We certainly can!

14 December

The Samaritan woman: sharing peace with strangers

Read JOHN 4:1–15

> **The Samaritan woman said to him, 'How is it that you, a Jew, ask a drink of me, a woman of Samaria?' (Jews do not share things in common with Samaritans.)**
> v. 9

Most of the encounters used as examples in this book have been of God's people in biblical times finding peace and, by implication, helping us to see how we as Christians might experience peace today. The story in today's passage turns the tables and reminds us that our mission is to announce and embody peace in the world and thereby enable others to share in it too.

This Samaritan woman was unlikely to have described her life as peaceful. She has often been portrayed, wrongly, as 'a loose woman', but we are given no details of why she had had five husbands. Did some die and others divorce her? Is there a story here of domestic violence, of drunkenness to the point where she could take no more? Is this the story of a woman with no living relatives, at the mercy of whoever came along next to offer her some protection and support, and in turn took advantage of her? We do not know, so we should not jump to any conclusions about her character.

But we do know that she expected little any more, and certainly not from a Jewish man at the well ahead of her. But he transformed her life, and so thorough was that transformation that she became an agent of transformation in the lives of others.

Is there a formula to follow here? Of course not. People are individuals and no programmatic approach can bring results. What stories give us is imagination, the ability to be inspired and in turn find the courage to live out our own version of the events before us. And this story is an inspiration, not least because it starts with low expectations yet takes so little to change so much.

Jesus asks for help. It's as simple as that. How often do we prefer to be the helper than the helped? Churches are very good at helping. Parents and toddlers, debt advice, rooms to hire at notional cost, gardens tidied up, invitations to carol services and mince pies, foodbanks – you name it, the church is good at it. But when did we ever ask for help? Even as individuals, we are often willing to help but less inclined to ask for it. There is something to learn here – it's not bad to ask for help when we need it.

Of course, our neighbours might be as surprised as the woman at the well. 'You're asking me for help?' But the conversation quickly turns from buckets and wells to matters of eternal significance. Isn't that a strange thought? That my neighbours might ever have given a thought to eternity, or to the limited years they have left, or to the meaning of the life they lead now. Surely not? Surely yes!

'But who am I to offer them spiritual advice?' you say. Don't offer them anything other than your story, and your story doesn't have to be dramatic, just authentic.

The disciples 'were astonished that he was speaking with a woman' (v. 27). I wonder how much of that is first-century Middle Eastern culture, and how much of it is a forerunner of our 21st-century non-Christian-aversion disorder! I speak as one who falls woefully short at this point. I have spent my working life inside a Christian mission, so must confess that almost all my friends are Christians. I sometimes wonder if my church friends would be equally astonished if they saw me speaking with someone who wasn't connected to church or mission. Some days I might astonish myself!

Back to the story and you'll never guess what happened next! But of course, you probably do know. She left the jar (suddenly the daily chores seemed less important) and ran off to tell others to come. They came, and they too decided to embrace the faith of this woman and become followers of Jesus. *Now* we're wishing this really *was* a formula, because this story ends so well. But different stories have different endings, and we can never be sure. It's best to be honest about that.

'Stay with us for a while,' they said, and Jesus stayed for two days. Imagine the joy of that time, and the endless questions; the sense of 'This is what we've been waiting for' and even more so, 'This is the one we've been waiting for.' When my faith came alive in my mid-20s, it all happened so quickly I was almost out of breath. But I could sum it up by saying that within the space of a few days I knew this was what I'd been looking for and who I was looking for.

I suspect this woman had not known peace since her childhood. We don't need to fabricate or imagine what her life had been like – let's just accept it was almost certainly dreadful. By now she was accustomed to her place in society and if anything felt it was only a matter of time before life dealt her another blow. But on this day, she found peace, and she did so through the least-expected person, a Jewish man.

For many of us the biggest barrier to reaching others with the good news of Jesus is our own inhibitions, our own nervousness, our own desire to be accepted and not rejected. Sometimes we have no expectation that others might want to know more about the person who one day transformed our lives. But we are very wrong in making these assumptions. There are countless people searching for meaning, for hope and for answers. And you might be the gateway to them. You could be the unexpected source of God's love touching their lives. Next time you need a bucket, go and ask your neighbour if you can borrow theirs.

15 December

Paul: peace in the face of death

Read PHILIPPIANS 1:15–26

> For to me, living is Christ and dying is gain. If I am to live in the flesh, that means fruitful labour for me; and I do not know which I prefer. I am hard pressed between the two: my desire is to depart and be with Christ, for that is far better; but to remain in the flesh is more necessary for you.
>
> vv. 21–24

I have enjoyed working with the poet Revd Lucy Berry for some years and come to value her wise and often humorous insights into the human condition. I asked her once to write a magazine article on dying well. She wrote the article, a brilliant piece, but summed up her views with the sentence, '[dying well] makes as much sense as being born badly. It suggests an independence, agency, autonomy which is not granted to us.' She is right, of course. We can't control how we die, though in case you're interested, I've put in a request for 'the peaceful passing in the night' option.

I do believe, however, that we can prepare for dying, or to face dying, in such a way that can bring us peace. Jesus was explicit in the promise he gave:

> Very truly, I tell you, anyone who hears my word and believes him who sent me has eternal life, and does not come under judgement, but has passed from death to life.
>
> JOHN 5:24

For the apostle Paul, to be 'in Christ' was the key, hence his affirmation that 'there is therefore now no condemnation for those who are in Christ Jesus' (Romans 8:1). So, to begin with, if you find yourself unsettled about death and dying, then these verses, and many others like them, can bring great confidence. That doesn't remove fear for everyone, because many of us simply fear the unknown, and death is certainly that.

For Paul, it would seem appropriate to say he was at peace even though he was in prison. 'To live is Christ and to die is gain' (v. 21, NIV) sounds like a win-win situation, and part of this positivity no doubt came from the fulfilment of seeing the gospel spread. Part of it too was because of the character of the man, able to rise above self-pity and say boldly, 'What has happened to me has actually helped to spread the gospel' (Philippians 1:12). But from a prison cell, that affirmation requires a deeper conviction, that no matter the circumstances he was able to live to the glory of Christ. Maybe that is why he could write to the Colossians, in another of his prison epistles:

> Set your minds on things that are above, not on things that are on earth, for you have died, and your life is hidden with Christ in God.
> COLOSSIANS 3:2–3

In those wonderful verses, he reminds us not only to live with one eye on the future, but in the meantime to know the ultimate security that is ours by faith. We have the Holy Spirit within us (1 Corinthians 6:19), and we are in Christ and Christ is in the Father.

Even when faith and our belief in heaven to come is largely settled, doubts can creep in. More than once, as I have sat with someone who knew the days of their life were ending, even when they had been a Christian for many years a sentiment would slip out along the lines of 'I haven't always lived a good life.' I understand that, and I would never brush it away. It's a human response, because we know that the standards for holy living are high and we are all too aware that we fall short. I reminded them that our inheritance is not linked in any way to how good we are. Romans 3:23 tells us 'all have sinned and fall short of the glory of God'; God is well aware of our shortcomings.

When Paul wrote to the Christians in Ephesus, he reminded them:

> By grace you have been saved through faith, and this is not your own doing; it is the gift of God – not the result of works, so that no one may boast.
> EPHESIANS 2:8–9

Isn't it interesting how many of us are better at giving gifts than receiving them? But the lesson here is clear – we must go on learning that God's love for us is unconditional. That's hard to understand, because most of the time our love of others isn't unconditional, but it's the truth we live by.

Then there are the regrets, the saddest of which has been when relationship issues have been left unresolved – parents estranged from children, siblings who haven't got along for years or, dare I say it, spouses who have left things unsaid between them. This is why it's best to say sorry quickly, even if you don't think you're at fault, whenever there is an argument or a misunderstanding. Paul also wrote to the Ephesians, 'do not let the sun go down on your anger' (Ephesians 4:26), because he knew it only becomes harder to say sorry with the passage of time as silence ensues, barriers get erected and positions become entrenched.

Sometimes it can be right to simply *say* you're sorry, but on occasion it can be better to write someone a note, maybe even post it. A note or letter that is handwritten, rather than sent electronically, can carry weight in a way that yet another email may not. It gives the recipient a chance to sit down and hold it, to read it a few times and to reflect on the extra effort taken in posting the mail, without the pressure to respond there and then. Extending an olive branch is an inherently physical thing.

Maybe your calling to be a peacemaker is to write a letter this week. Offer forgiveness, if needed; ask for it, if that is more appropriate. Life is too short to leave these things undone, and it gets shorter with each passing day.

16 December

Peter: peace in times of change

Read ACTS 10:1–48

> Peter went up on the roof to pray. He became hungry and
> wanted something to eat; and while it was being prepared, he
> fell into a trance. He saw the heaven opened and something
> like a large sheet coming down, being lowered to the ground
> by its four corners.
>
> vv. 9–11

If ever there was a complex character it is our beloved Peter. He was
eager and impulsive, quick to speak, sometimes slow to learn. He
was the first of the apostles to affirm that Jesus was the Messiah
(Mark 8:29) but subsequently denied ever being with him (Mark
14:68). He objected to Jesus wanting to wash his feet, then asked
him to wash his whole body (John 13:9). He was forgiven by Jesus,
when Jesus asked him three times, 'Do you love me?' (John 21:15),
yet moments later seemed preoccupied with asking Jesus, 'What
about him?' in reference to the beloved disciple, likely the apostle
John (John 21:21).

Peter was loveable and frustrating in equal measure, a reminder
if it was needed that Jesus has no requirement for perfect people
to be his disciples. For all his faults, Peter was someone Jesus
entrusted much to. While we read a lot about Paul throughout the
New Testament, largely because it comprises so many of Paul's
letters, Peter too was clearly among the leading apostles, and the
early chapters of Acts feature Peter in a prominent leading role. He
was there when the Holy Spirit came upon the disciples (Acts 2) and
preached thunderous sermons (Acts 2—4). He was among the first
disciples to be arrested, saw the first converts (Acts 2:37–42), healed

a crippled man (Acts 3) and even brought the dead Tabitha back to life (Acts 9:40). The power of God was rampant, and Peter was at the heart of it.

Then came the astonishing encounter with Cornelius. The story is told twice, first in Acts 10 and then also in Acts 11 when Peter defends himself in Jerusalem, with the outcome decided in the church council in Acts 15. It's hard for us to grasp the magnitude of what Peter was being asked to embrace. After nearly 1,800 years, from Abram to that day, the people of Israel knew that in God's eyes they were his chosen people and one day a Messiah would come. But now Peter was being told that the gospel was not just for Jewish people but for all who believed in Jesus – Jews and Gentiles alike. The church is now the chosen people. Furthermore, much of the Old Testament laws, which had taught and guided them till now (Galatians 3:23–26), needed to be laid upon the shoulders of the Gentiles. This was revolutionary!

Sudden or huge change affects our equilibrium. A redundancy or a health scare shocks us. Even positive changes like falling in love or moving location will affect us. What was solid is suddenly fluid. What was predictable is now uncertain. Because of these things we do all we can to reinstate solidity and predictability as soon as possible. Even among those who like change, there is a recognition that permanent change is exhausting and even troubling.

Years ago I was excited and hungry for more of God. Today, nearly four decades on, do I still have that desire? I hope so. Have you a desire to be shown new things, to be encouraged to examine previously held convictions, to take on a new cause for the sake of Christ, recapturing the eagerness of younger years as best you can?

All around us the world is crying out for God's people to engage or re-engage and be Christ's hands, feet and voice in the public square. Irrespective of political affiliation, are we concerned for the poor in our town – for those who need help from food banks to get to the end of the week? Those who are homeless or on drugs or in debt? Is there a lurking suspicion in your heart or mine that these people just didn't work hard enough – in short, they just don't deserve it? But then we remember that neither did we deserve the love of Christ.

Social norms have changed too. How do we relate to those who live together and choose to get married later or not at all? Those who are gay, both Christians and non-Christians? What about economic migrants? I'm one of the latter; my family came from Ireland in 1960 looking for a better life. Being Irish wasn't easy in the 1960s and 1970s, the years of 'the troubles', when 'No Blacks, No Dogs, No Irish' could sometimes be seen in landlords' windows. Today's outsiders are eastern Europeans, refugees from Syria and Afghanistan, and economic migrants from Africa. Isn't it strange that we don't call someone who goes to New York from the City to work in a bank an economic migrant? Our language says a lot about us.

I'm aware of the political, social, theological and ethical issues these subjects raise. But I don't think any reasons exist for failing to reach out in compassion to help those in need, whether that need is for a home, acceptance, a job or simply our understanding.

How would Jesus respond? Surely he would do so with compassion, and probably in such a way that his response would make us as uncomfortable as Peter was when Jesus wanted to wash his feet or when he heard that voice pronouncing all kinds of unclean animals as clean.

Around the same time as Peter's vision, Cornelius also had a vision, and he sent for the apostle. When the two met the Holy Spirit fell upon them, Jews and Gentiles alike, and Peter baptised the household of Cornelius. As Peter said, 'I truly understand that God shows no partiality' (Acts 10:34).

Did Peter find peace through this period of tumultuous change? Yes, he did. He reported the whole matter to the church in Jerusalem and proclaimed, 'If then God gave them the same gift that he gave us when we believed in the Lord Jesus Christ, who was I that I could hinder God?' (Acts 11:17). The others were silenced. The church was changed!

All around us today society is changing too, and we have to respond. What might God be saying to us today that is as revolutionary as that which he revealed to Peter?

Part III

The Prince of Peace

17 December

For unto us is born a child

Read ISAIAH 9:2–7

> For a child has been born for us,
>   a son given to us;
> authority rests upon his shoulders;
>   and he is named
> Wonderful Counsellor, Mighty God,
>   Everlasting Father, Prince of Peace.
>
> v. 6

Waiting for the birth of a child, especially a first child, is a wait like no other: a room to be set aside and decorated, a buggy to be purchased and all sorts of plans to be made, from what sort of clothes to get and what colours to choose. On a more reflective level, parents wonder about what the child will be like and how the life of the child might work out.

Imagine if the wait was for hundreds of years rather than nine months, and a whole nation was waiting rather than just the parents. The world's cameras outside a hospital in London waiting for news of the royal baby would be nothing compared to this! And how strange would it be if the parents weren't even known? The expectations would be there, but no one would really know where to look. And the expectations were extraordinary. This child would be nothing less than the saviour of the people, the one who would rid us of all our worries and fears. That really would be a waiting period like no other.

This describes the situation among God's people over many generations. As their strength waxed and waned, as their relationship with God ebbed and flowed, through it all like a golden thread there was the hope of a Messiah, a Saviour, one who would be the anointed of God and who would bring peace into their troubled lives.

Living expectantly is a good thing. From an early age we have ideas of what we want to be when we grow up. We often make career choices based on a vision of how we want to use our gifts. We know that our choices shape our future and that awareness is something we shouldn't lose as we grow older. Friends, family, homes and jobs will quickly inhabit the spaces of our lives, and we can lose any sense of 'Where does God want to be in ten years' time?' or 'Am I using my gifts to the full?'

Alongside this expectancy about my own life, there is also a much bigger picture of which we are a small but not insignificant part. How is my generation responding to the call of God? Where is God's Spirit evidently on the move? Where do we see the blatant injustices in today's world? And in response to these, what role might God be asking me to play?

The people of Israel had day-to-day and year-to-year hopes like the rest of us, but they also had a big-picture hope, one that focused on their relationship as a people to God. The equivalent for us today would be the church as the people of God; not simply my local church or yours, but the church that encompasses all of God's people, in all places, in all times.

Just as Israel longed for the coming of their Messiah, we are encouraged to long for Jesus' return. Just after the ascension of Jesus, the angels asked the disciples, 'Why do you stand here looking into the sky? This same Jesus, who has been taken up from you into heaven, will come in the same way as you saw him go into heaven' (Acts 1:11). And the penultimate verse of the Bible says, 'Amen. Come Lord Jesus!' (Revelation 22:20).

That yearning is for us focused on Jesus, for we know him to be the Messiah that Israel once longed for. Therefore, during this waiting period we should be putting into place the plan that Jesus has for the world. Put simply, if Jesus is our 'Wonderful Counsellor, Mighty God, Everlasting Father, Prince of Peace' (v. 6), we should be hoping to shape the world to reflect these great traits.

Wonderful Counsellor is perhaps best understood as supernatural counsellor and tells us that the wisdom of God is revealed to us in Jesus through the pages of the New Testament, through prayer and through the indwelling guidance of the Holy Spirit. This wisdom should be our guiding light for living, and we should seek to share this with others.

Mighty God reminds us of our worshipful relationship to Jesus. He is the one true God, born in the flesh. The attitude of the Christmas visitors to the newborn child is a reminder that one day everyone will bow the knee before him. But more than that, our behaviour, lifestyle, priorities and attitudes will betray whether our worship is truly of the heart or something less genuine.

Everlasting Father can be confusing at first glance, as we see this as a prophecy about Jesus. But the nature of the Messiah that Israel longed for was the one who would care for and protect his people as a father would do over his tribe or clan. God is, in Christ, the Father of all humankind – he cares for the helpless. The Psalms describe God as 'A father to the fatherless, a defender of widows' (Psalm 68:5, NIV).

Prince of Peace is, as we have seen, the title that captures the heart of Israel's longing. As we saw in the reflection for 3 December, 'peace' represents everything from fruitful harvests to safety from the enemy. But peace with God was Israel's longing too – to know that God's face was turned towards them. In another wonderful messianic passage, we read that 'the punishment that brought us peace was on him' (Isaiah 53:5, NIV).

In our lives, therefore – in these 'waiting for Jesus to return' years – we do well to put these characteristics into practice; to live a worshipful life such that all we do and say and are becoming bears witness to the one we say we are following; to offer Jesus to an unbelieving world as the one in whom all truth is found; to care for the weak and the helpless as they will be cared for in the renewed heaven and renewed earth of God's kingdom; and to live as peacemakers at all times, something we will take up in the final section of the book.

18 December

But you, Bethlehem...

Read MICAH 5:2–5

> 'But you, Bethlehem Ephrathah,
>   though you are small among the clans of Judah,
> out of you will come for me
>   one who will be ruler over Israel,
> whose origins are from of old,
>   from ancient times.'
>
> v. 2 (NIV)

Everyone loves an underdog. Whether it's Susan Boyle wowing the nation on *Britain's Got Talent* in 2009 (and becoming an international superstar) or Eddie 'The Eagle' Edwards competing in the 1988 Winter Olympics (and becoming a global celebrity), there has long been a fascination with those who come from humble beginnings to achieve great things. Of course, the fascination only exists because the upstart is usually mocked or derided (think of David standing before Goliath) or they get what they deserve – in sport usually a whopping defeat. But sometimes, just sometimes, the underdog wins! That's what captures our imagination. Nathaniel's remark, 'Nazareth! Can anything good come from there?' (John 1:46, NIV), is evidence that no one is exempt from the possibility of a good put-down!

When Micah first gave his prophecy, Jerusalem was under siege and the people of Judah longed for deliverance and a peaceful life. Unlike Jerusalem, with its magnificent buildings and famed importance, Bethlehem was truly the local village, 'small among the clans of Judah' (v. 2). But Bethlehem had its own claim to fame. It was the home of Jesse, the father of David, Israel's greatest king (1 Samuel

17:12), so there is more than a suggestion here that the long-awaited ruler would be another David.

This passage reveals a deep truth about how God works. James Limburg in his commentary on Micah makes the point well:

> We recognise a biblical theme here: God's choice of the least likely, the littlest to accomplish God's purposes. Thus Gideon declared himself to be from the weakest clan, and the youngest in the family (Judges 6:15), Saul described his tribe as amongst the 'least' of those in Israel (1 Samuel 9:21). The Lord chose David, the youngest, over his brothers (1 Samuel 16:1–13). The theme finds climactic expression in the announcement that the Messiah and Saviour of the world is the baby lying in the manger (Luke 2).[2]

The New Testament continues this theme with Jesus' parables, such as that which likens the kingdom of God to a mustard seed (Matthew 13:31–32), and other teaching, such as how even a tiny amount of faith can move mountains (Matthew 17:20). Jesus not only taught that the least shall be the greatest and the greatest shall be the least (see, for example, Luke 9:48), he also enacted it on the night of the Passover as he washed the feet of his disciples (John 13:12).

These illustrations serve to remind us of something important about our faith. In personal terms, we should never write off the impact we can make as individuals. Maybe you long to see your family or friends come to faith and yet you feel powerless. Perhaps in your community you see something that should be changed but wonder who will do it. The old saying that 'the person who thinks they're too small to make a difference has never shared a bed with a mosquito' is a timely reminder of the power of determination to achieve great things. William Carey, Hudson Taylor, Ida Scudder, Rosa Parks and Martin Luther King Jr stand in a long list of men and women who have achieved mighty deeds in Christ's name. I wonder if there are changes you see around you that seem insurmountable.

The same is true of the church in the UK today. In 2017, the *Guardian* reported that 48% of the UK is now avowedly non-Christian.[3] That is a depressing statistic, but frankly it didn't disturb me. I don't mean that I welcomed it or that I didn't lament it, but that it only confirmed what would have been my assumption. I have worked in countries where the Christian community was a single-figure percentage of the population, and news of just a few people coming to faith was celebrated. Over the years, if we could place five or six missionaries in a city of millions, we believed we could make a real difference. In the UK, if I'm speaking in a church of 50 people who are nostalgic for the days when they were 100 or more, I often remind them that tomorrow morning they will be deploying 50 missionaries to work in their town. With God on our side we can see things differently. It all depends on where you start from. So don't despair about the church in the west; Christ is the head of the church (Colossians 1:18), and he has taken care of his people through years of persecution, spiritual drought and famine, and cultural dislocation.

This prophecy of Micah is important, and it neatly fits the Christmas story. Matthew quotes the prophecy as part of his telling of the birth of Christ, contrasting the weakness of a newborn infant from the nowhere village of Bethlehem with the might of Herod, who was 'frightened' at the news of the child's birth (Matthew 2:3–6). Herod's reaction suggests that Micah's prophecy had wide acceptance in those days and that the sense of expectation had grown. With the testimony of the shepherds spreading and news of an angelic visitation reaching Jerusalem, we see the power of the good news of Jesus affecting even the seemingly powerful forces arraigned against it.

Part of our Christian tradition is the annual retelling of these events, and that retelling keeps the narrative alive. If you have people visiting your church for the once-a-year carol service and you are tempted to think, 'Huh! Bet we won't see them again before next year', don't you dare! Sowing the seeds of the Christmas story is vital, and maybe one day soon God will reap what is sown – and the 48% might just think again.

19 December

Annunciation

LUKE 1:26–38

In the sixth month the angel Gabriel was sent by God to a town in Galilee called Nazareth, to a virgin engaged to a man whose name was Joseph, of the house of David. The virgin's name was Mary. And he came to her and said, 'Greetings, favoured one! The Lord is with you.' But she was much perplexed by his words and pondered what sort of greeting this might be. The angel said to her, 'Do not be afraid, Mary, for you have found favour with God. And now, you will conceive in your womb and bear a son, and you will name him Jesus. He will be great, and will be called the Son of the Most High, and the Lord God will give to him the throne of his ancestor David. He will reign over the house of Jacob for ever, and of his kingdom there will be no end.' Mary said to the angel, 'How can this be, since I am a virgin?' The angel said to her, 'The Holy Spirit will come upon you, and the power of the Most High will overshadow you; therefore the child to be born will be holy; he will be called Son of God. And now, your relative Elizabeth in her old age has also conceived a son; and this is the sixth month for her who was said to be barren. For nothing will be impossible with God.' Then Mary said, 'Here am I, the servant of the Lord; let it be with me according to your word.' Then the angel departed from her.

Like many baby boomers, my early years have left me with many precious memories of wonderful children's TV programmes. Among them was the programme *How*, which ran from 1966 to 1981 and sought to explain how different things worked or were made. The show never addressed the birth of Christ, though asking 'How?'

would certainly be an understandable reaction to the news that a virgin would have a child. Indeed, if ever there was a message likely to unsettle its recipient, the announcement Mary received was it. Now the drama really begins.

The angel Gabriel brings news to Mary that will change both her life and the history of the world. In keeping with yesterday's theme, here we see God putting his audacious salvation plan to work in a most unlikely way. An unknown girl, betrothed to a man called Joseph but whose union has not yet been consummated, is chosen. From our perspective, God's plan raises so many questions. There is both a *problem* – how does a virgin give birth – and a *mystery* – she is called 'the favoured one' and told 'the Lord is with you'.

First, the *problem*, namely of how – or to use Mary's words, 'How can this be?' (v. 34). Over the years some have said that this story of the virgin birth is unlikely to be true, and if we're speaking of 'likelihood' then such a view is correct. But is 'How likely is it?' the best tool of discernment we can bring to our consideration of God? Is that how we should judge the works of God? 'Is it likely?' Of course, it isn't! Since when is God restricted to doing what is likely? Surely if our faith is in the God who created the heavens and the earth; who healed the sick and forgave sinners; who gave sight to the blind and restored the legs of a paralysed man; who calmed a storm and turned water into wine, then the virgin birth, far from presenting us with a problem, instead challenges us to move away from our human preoccupation with 'How?' and ask instead 'Why?'

The former question is always our preferred one because it expresses domination. 'Tell me how; explain yourself' puts us in the upper seat with our demand for an answer. And it works wonderfully, especially in the area of scientific exploration, without which our lives would be so much poorer. But science knows its limits, and men and women need to know their limits too. Moreover, we assume we would understand the answer, when I think God laughs at these moments knowing that we couldn't even begin to understand the 'how'.

But when we ask 'Why?' we encounter *mystery*, and rightly place ourselves in a subordinate role. There is usually no unwillingness to reveal the 'why'. To garner that insight, we must recall the multiple prophecies in the Old Testament, including Isaiah 7:14 ('The virgin will conceive and give birth to a son, and will call him Immanuel', NIV); Isaiah 11:6–9; the four servant songs (Isaiah 42:1–7; 49:1–6; 50:4–9; 52:13—53:12); and Micah 5:2. The generations-long hunger for the Messiah was part of the DNA of God's people. These prophecies begin to answer the big question 'Why?', or at least 'Why Mary?'

A further reason is contained in the words of the angel, 'The Lord is with you.' We said at the outset of these reflections that the secret to peace – for ourselves but surely also for our world – is the presence of God. Here we have a foreshadowing of the birth of the Christ child – Gabriel is saying God is with you now; in other words, his favour is with you, his face is towards you and his blessing rests upon you. But soon, the child you will bear, conceived of the Holy Spirit, will be Immanuel – God with us. And lest we think Joseph was simply a forlorn bystander, verse 27 shows that he was a descendant of David, from Bethlehem. The union of Mary and Joseph was, as you'd expect, perfect.

Take in the enormity of what is said to Mary. That she would conceive by the Holy Spirit is one thing. To also hear that your child 'will be great and will be called the Son of the Most High' (v. 32); that he will have 'the throne of his ancestor David' (v. 32); that 'he will reign over the house of Jacob for ever' (v. 33); that 'of his kingdom will be no end' (v. 33); and – wait for it – 'he will called Son of God' (v. 35) – it's a wonder Mary didn't pass out.

But instead she responded according to her deep and trusting faith: 'Here am I, the servant of the Lord; let it be with me according to your word.' Act 1, scene 1 is complete.

20 December

Mary visits Elizabeth

LUKE 1:39–45 (NIV)

> At that time Mary got ready and hurried to a town in the hill country of Judea, where she entered Zechariah's home and greeted Elizabeth. When Elizabeth heard Mary's greeting, the baby leaped in her womb, and Elizabeth was filled with the Holy Spirit. In a loud voice she exclaimed: 'Blessed are you among women, and blessed is the child you will bear! But why am I so favoured, that the mother of my Lord should come to me? As soon as the sound of your greeting reached my ears, the baby in my womb leaped for joy. Blessed is she who has believed that the Lord would fulfil his promises to her!'

Most men, if they are honest, envy the closeness women often share together. Not all women, of course, but many do, be they sisters, cousins, school friends or work mates. Men have friendships too, but they are less intimate, more arm's length. Mary was told that Elizabeth was pregnant and set off to be with her, no doubt with the thought of offering support to her older cousin, but surely too because it was an opportunity to talk with someone she loved about the news the angel had brought. Elizabeth was also known for her godliness (Luke 1:6) and surely over the years there had been forged a deep connection between her and Mary. Elizabeth had wanted a child for years; now God had blessed her. Mary too had been blessed by God but in different circumstances. Two women; two babies; two interconnected lives; and, let it be said, two heart-breaking deaths in the years ahead.

In terms of the peace that we are exploring, Elizabeth found it after years of yearning, but the life of her son would not always bring peace to her, especially if she lived to see his end. The peace of God, as we have said, is multifaceted. Here it brought her joy, but it did not insulate her from the sorrows to come. Mary's experience was the same – her heartache was unspeakable. Did she have the peace of God at Calvary? That would be to ask too much, to engage in mere sentimentalism. There are times when we walk the disciple's road devoid of the peace we once had and that we long to return.

Elizabeth's understanding of the significance of the gift of her unborn son, relayed to her from Zechariah in spite of his inability to speak (Luke 1:20), meant that in the moment she glimpsed Mary (and her baby leapt in her womb) she made the connection between herself and Mary, and between their two children. Elizabeth and Mary were surely in harmony with God's own heart. Nonetheless, there is deep mystery here also. How did she know that Mary was blessed among women, and Mary's baby was her Lord (v. 43)? Perhaps our only clue is her exclamation, 'Blessed is she who has believed that the Lord would fulfil his promises to her!' (v. 45).

Elizabeth's and Mary's faith create the human dimension of this story. Their faith meets God's purposes, and God's will is done. In our longing for that peace we have been studying, we must consider that it may not drop into our laps like a celestial gift. It is, for sure, a gift, not something earned or merited. But grace allows room for our participation; God allows space for our free will. Some will dispute this, preferring the view that God's will can never be thwarted, and there is a theological debate to be had about that. But if God's will is predetermined, such that we do not really have the free choice to accept or reject, participate or ignore, then it seems to me to make for a lesser God, and a lesser relationship with God.

Elizabeth and Mary are shining examples to us precisely because they were devoted to God and willingly embraced God's will for their lives. Mary's 'May your word to me be fulfilled' (Luke 1:38, NIV) and

Elizabeth's 'Blessed is she who has believed that the Lord would fulfil his promises to her!' (v. 45) express their free response to God's invitation to participate in the outworking of his will. Much is said these days about 'the mission of God' as a counter to 'the mission of the church', the point being that God is active in salvation history long before we join in. When we talk of unreached people groups, we can only mean unreached *by us*, because there is no place or no peoples unreached by God. Like Mary and Elizabeth, what is required of us is not to dream up a mission strategy but to participate in God's mission strategy, which is precisely what these two women did. God's will was revealed to them and they responded with their willing obedience.

Mary's spoken response is captured beautifully in the prayer we call the Magnificat, to which we turn next. But lest we forget the very human, very warm nature of Mary's journey to her cousin, spare a moment to consider what their three months together would have been like. They would have talked and worked together, Mary doing some of the chores that Elizabeth might now be finding difficult. And the big question – did Mary stay for the birth? She stayed with Elizabeth for three months (Luke 1:56), which would have been to the full term of Elizabeth's pregnancy, so surely she must have, but that isn't made clear.

21 December

The Magnificat: Mary's song

LUKE 1:46–56 (NIV)

And Mary said:

'My soul glorifies the Lord
    and my spirit rejoices in God my Saviour,
for he has been mindful
    of the humble state of his servant.
From now on all generations will call me blessed,
    for the Mighty One has done great things for me – holy is
    his name.
His mercy extends to those who fear him,
    from generation to generation.
He has performed mighty deeds with his arm;
    he has scattered those who are proud in their inmost
    thoughts.
He has brought down rulers from their thrones
    but has lifted up the humble.
He has filled the hungry with good things
    but has sent the rich away empty.
He has helped his servant Israel,
    remembering to be merciful
to Abraham and his descendants for ever,
    just as he promised our ancestors.'

Mary stayed with Elizabeth for about three months and then
returned home.

When my wider family get together – usually at Christmas and for
weddings and funerals – we share stories, and we tease each other

as the old tales get told and retold. In the act of retelling, they are passed from one generation to another. Occasionally details emerge years later that others hadn't known and so a more comprehensive picture emerges. Given that today's technology offers us more ways than ever to pass on and store information, it is a wonder that the oral tradition is still so important.

In Mary's time, this orality was even more important precisely because of the absence of alternatives. We sometimes forget that the accounts of the life of Christ were compiled years after the events they describe. They would have been put together from multiple conversations, with details added by different voices, questions asked and answers given, and the writer then weaving them together into a semblance of order. What has emerged is nevertheless trust-worthy because of the many voices that have contributed to the process, each adding detail, colour, texture and insight into the tale. Not all accounts will be the same, itself a mark of the authentic recollection of different sources.

Mary and Elizabeth would have remembered their meeting and how each responded to the other. It's possible most of this remembrance, Mary's song, came from Elizabeth, as she likely was asked in later life, 'What happened when Mary came to see you?' Mary too would have shared the details of the story of these early days, of the angelic appearance. Joseph would have confirmed that their union was not consummated before their son was born.

The language and structure of the song is telling. Many of the words allude to passages from, and the composition is akin to the poetry of, the Old Testament. Certainly there is a resemblance to Hannah's prayer (1 Samuel 2:1–10). This is not surprising given the oral tradition of Mary's culture. How else was a village girl to express her praise to God other than through the patterns and prayers she had been steeped in since childhood? Her familiarity with ancient texts used to praise God meant that she adopted their form in order to do likewise.

Perhaps there is a learning point for us in this, that if we have a ready acquaintance with the scriptures, we too will find patterns and prayers for conveying who we are in the light of God's relationship to us, ways of expressing our joys and sorrows, and at a deeper level our uncertainties and doubts. We have ready examples in our culture, such as the widespread familiarity with the Lord's Prayer and the annual repetition of Christmas carols. These continue to pass on the tradition and provide the language, even to a largely unchurched generation, with which to express something deep inside.

Mary's song is beautiful in its structure and expression. She is keenly aware of her uniqueness, but her words direct praise to God and away from any sense of self-aggrandisement. Her soul magnifies her Lord and she acknowledges that God is her Saviour (vv. 46–47). The word 'rejoices' (v. 47) is one of ecstasy, of great exultation, a reflection of the enormity of what is happening to her, amplified by the gulf between her 'humble state' and the knowledge that now 'generations will call me blessed' (v. 48). Even then, she would not have fully realised what this meant – her thoughts of generations were likely limited only to Israel, not the global faith that Christianity has become since her lifetime.

Quickly Mary's focus again turns to God, who 'has done great things for me', a sign of God's great mercy (vv. 49–50). Verses 51–53 are complex in the original language – it is debatable whether they are to be interpreted as speaking of God's action in the past, God's action in the future or God's habitual action. Given what we know of God, we can say with some certainty that it is all three. We know enough about God and God's kingdom to know that he scatters the proud, brings down rulers, lifts the humble, feeds the hungry and sends the rich away empty. Indeed, the ministry of Jesus exemplified these traits too, as we would expect. Care must be taken, however, for these are not simplistic categories. Rulers who rule with justice or the rich who use their wealth to bless others are not in view here, and there is a false humility that is manipulative of others and which is not an attractive or a godly trait. Mary's point in these verses, however, is surely to expand on the mercy of God mentioned in verse 50. The very things that deprive people of life in all its fullness – abuse of power, injustice, poverty – are the elements that will be overturned in God's kingdom.

The final two verses of the song are important, as they locate Mary's self-reflection in the grand sweep of history that stretches back to God's covenant with Abraham, the father of the nation, to whom was given the promise 'I will make your offspring like the dust of the earth, so that if anyone could count the dust, then your offspring could be counted' (Genesis 13:16, NIV). And in Genesis 15:5 we read, '[The Lord] took [Abram] outside and said, "Look up at the sky and count the stars – if indeed you can count them." Then he said to him, "So shall your offspring be."'

As you read today's passage with faith, however strong or weak that faith is, you are part of that great throng of descendants that Mary envisaged, that God had promised to Abraham and that Jesus came to gather to himself.

22 December

John the Baptist

Read LUKE 1:57–79

And you, my child, will be called a prophet of the Most High;
    for you will go on before the Lord to prepare the way for him,
to give his people the knowledge of salvation
    through the forgiveness of their sins,
because of the tender mercy of our God,
    by which the rising sun will come to us from heaven
to shine on those living in darkness
    and in the shadow of death,
to guide our feet into the path of peace.'
vv. 76–79 (NIV)

If you have ever held a newborn baby in your arms, especially if the child is your own, you will perhaps have spoken some hushed words to him or her, away from others. 'Well, hello. I'm your mum (or dad, auntie, uncle)!' I did so with my newborn children; they were precious moments when I said something like, 'I'm your dad, and I'm wondering what life holds for you. What kind of person will you be?' And I'll have added, 'Your mum and I will be there for you.' Yes, our daughters were possibly asleep and certainly uncomprehending, but the significance of that chat is not who hears it but the speaking of it. This is the moment when the latent potential of a new life becomes real. You actually have that little bundle in your arms and their story has begun.

The appearance of the angel to Zechariah (Luke 1:11), announcing Elizabeth's late-in-life conception and the subsequent birth of John, who became known as the Baptist, are events closely connected to the birth of Jesus. The fulfilment of Old Testament prophecies (e.g.

Isaiah 40:3–5) relating to one who would go before the Messiah was a key part of God's unfolding plan.

There was a fuss on the eighth day, when the baby was brought to the temple, because the relatives thought John was a strange name – not one that was used in their family – but Elizabeth and Zechariah were adamant. That was what the angel had said! Zechariah's tongue was then loosened (he had been unable to talk after seeing the angel; see Luke 1:20) and he uttered a wonderful song to God (vv. 67–79).

Zechariah's prayer praises God and recounts, like Mary before him, that God is fulfilling the promise he gave to Abraham. Through the prompting of the Spirit he sees that this child, when full grown, will travel and call people to get ready for God, who was doing a new thing. He would call people to prepare for the Messiah, and he would baptise them so their sins would be forgiven. Later Jesus was also baptised by John (Matthew 3:13; Mark 1:9; Luke 3:21), not because he needed forgiveness but as an act of identification with those whose place he would take on the cross at the end of his earthly life.

All this future is captured in Zechariah's 'dad moment', as he cradled his son and whispered the words from today's passage (Luke 1:76–79).

The phrase from the final verse – 'to guide our feet into the path of peace' – is a poetic reminder that there are many ways that the purposes of God can be expressed. Our task today is also to be guides pointing towards the Lord, and we can be helped in this by seeing how different approaches help people see their need of God. Each can bring different dimensions of understanding. For example, a call to repent can really hit home in the life of someone who is openly rebelling against a godly way of life, but it won't necessarily be the best way to approach everyone at first. God is not only the forgiver of sins; he is also the healer, and damaged people need to know that. He is the embracing parent of the prodigal son or daughter who wonder whether there is a path back home (see Luke 15). To those in turmoil, he is the one who calms the storm. To those who have been defeated by life, he is the one who gets us to our feet and helps us walk once more. To those who hunger for something deeper and thirst after righteousness, he is the bread of life and the living water. To those who fear death or are facing death or wonder about life after death, he is the resurrection and the life.

There are hundreds of ways of describing God and his salvation (and preachers especially have a responsibility to paint the full canvas of God's character). To know them all requires a close familiarity with scripture, but arguably they are all summed up by the phrase 'to guide our feet into the path of peace'. For as we have seen, to be at peace is to be forgiven and healed and restored – and loved and embraced and fed and adopted and given the promise of life eternal, and a thousand more things beside!

In that moment when Zechariah gazed upon his child, he foresaw all of this and more. Within a few months the Saviour of the world would be born to Mary, and this little child in his arms would play a key role in the fulfilment of God's purposes.

23 December

The journey

LUKE 2:1-5 (NIV)

> In those days Caesar Augustus issued a decree that a census
> should be taken of the entire Roman world. (This was the first
> census that took place while Quirinius was governor of Syria.)
> And everyone went to their own town to register. So Joseph
> also went up from the town of Nazareth in Galilee to Judea,
> to Bethlehem the town of David, because he belonged to the
> house and line of David. He went there to register with Mary,
> who was pledged to be married to him and was expecting
> a child.

Chris Rea's wonderful song 'Driving Home for Christmas' is played
in our house several times in the days running up to Christmas.
This is especially so if our children are on the way – if it comes on
the radio (and it always does), I'll call them and make sure they're
listening to it! The song captures the happiness and excitement of
the season.

Christmas is a time of travel for many – to be in the right place, with
the right people, at the right time. This was a feature of Christmas
from the beginning, as Mary and Joseph set off for Bethlehem,
despite her being heavily pregnant. The journey would have been
arduous, the nights cold and overnight accommodation something
of a lottery. Nonetheless the place – Bethlehem – was right; the time
was right; and getting Mary there was right. This was what in the
Bible is called *kairos* – a God-ordained moment in time.

I believe that Mary and Joseph were aware of this. Remember that
an angel had appeared to Mary at the annunciation (Luke 1:26) and

to Joseph later (Matthew 1:20), explaining what was happening. They both believed what the angel had said, as evidenced by their responses (Luke 1:38; Matthew 1:24). As a result they would have spoken much about the significance of what was happening to them. It is almost certain that they would have worked out that by going to Bethlehem for the census they were moving into line with the prophecy that spoke of the Messiah being born there (Micah 5:2). Similarly, they would have heard in the synagogue since they were small about Isaiah's prophecy of the miraculous conception (Isaiah 7:14), so as unbelievable as it might have seemed, maybe the angels were indeed who they said they were. Remember too that, like many people in the global south today, their belief in the active presence of God in their lives made the occurrence of miracles far less problematic than it is for those of us who have been anaesthetised to the power of God by so-called rational thinking.

We know from Mary's song in Luke 1 that she was well-versed in the Old Testament, and there's no reason to think Joseph wasn't also devout, even if the evidence is less explicit. So we can imagine their excitement, and fear, as they began to piece together a remarkable picture, even if it is most unlikely that they understood the fullness of what we now know. They would have recalled the promises to Abraham, the entry into the promised land, the years of captivity in Egypt and later in exile. Even now the domination by Roman occupiers made them yearn for deliverance. Maybe, just maybe, they were chosen by God to be at the heart of this story. They chose to believe, and so they were obedient to what appeared to be God's leading, not least because it was consistent with the holy scriptures.

Here we have an important lesson for our own lives, and especially for the perennial questions that emerge around the subject of God's guidance, from the small ('What should I do now?') to the great ('What is happening to our world today?'). These were Mary's and Joseph's questions too, and I can detect four ways in which their response can help us.

First, nurture a living relationship with God. Mary's response to Gabriel and her evident devoutness underlines why she was chosen by God to bear the Messiah. We're told also that Joseph was 'a righteous man' (Matthew 1:19), and we see something of his character when in the same verse we read that he was 'unwilling to expose her to public disgrace'.

Second, and contributing to the above, know your scriptures. Mary and Joseph's reactions to the angelic encounters were laced with scriptural references, but just as importantly, their familiarity with God's story will have helped them locate what was happening to them within God's unfolding plan. We too live at a time in history when God's plans are still unfolding. We live in a time between the ascension and the return of Christ, when God's invitation to us is to participate in the outworking of his purposes spoken of in passages such as Matthew 25:31–46, 28:19–20 and John 20:21. We live in a time of great upheaval, with everything from untold wealth to unspeakable poverty; with millions being on the move and billions being made by the uber-rich; with the challenge of globalisation and climate change. We need Christians to be involved in business, public services, charities, the arts and, over all of them, politics. Where in scripture do we find the encouragement and challenge to address these issues?

Third, believe in the God for whom nothing is impossible. We can be devout and know our Bible, but we can set our horizon so near that we see God as just a slightly better version of ourselves. A key part of Mary's response to the angel is her acceptance of Gabriel's assertion that 'nothing will be impossible with God' (Luke 1:37). She had her questions – 'How can this be, since I am a virgin?' (Luke 1:34) – but she nevertheless chose to believe. Are there areas in your life where you long for God to work but actually have decided that nothing will happen? Meditate on this – to believe nothing is impossible is an act of the will, an act of deep faith in God.

And fourth, Mary and Joseph stepped out in faith. The real test is when we say, 'Lord, here I am. Let's get to work!' Mary accepted what was happening to her even though she was truly afraid. Joseph was minded to leave her but stayed. They put their knowledge of scripture and their belief in the God of the impossible into practice and they set off for Bethlehem. Is there something in your life where you need to step out and ask God to show you the way?

Chris Rea, in his song mentioned earlier, sings of getting home to 'get my feet on holy ground'. That was where Mary and Joseph were heading too.

24 December

The Word became flesh

Read PHILIPPIANS 2:5–11

Let the same mind be in you that was in Christ Jesus, who, though he was in the form of God, did not regard equality with God as something to be exploited, but emptied himself, taking the form of a slave, being born in human likeness.

vv. 5–7

So far our story has been about people. From Adam and Eve to Mary and Joseph, they and a host of others stand in the mainstream of this unfolding story. But for a moment, on the eve of Christmas, we turn our thoughts to God. It's easy to portray God's role in heroic terms as simply that of Saviour or Redeemer. Little is said about how the incarnation affected God, because nothing about God can be known unless it is revealed. But there are clues dotted around. Jesus grew in knowledge and understanding as a child (Luke 2:52), and later we know he grieved (John 11:38), wept (John 11:35), was thirsty (John 4:7), was angry (Mark 3:5), loved (Mark 10:21), and on the cross cried to his Father, 'Why have you forsaken me?' (Matthew 27:46). In these verses and more we get glimpses, only glimpses, of what it meant for Jesus to become flesh and live among us.

In today's passage from the apostle Paul's letter to the Philippians, where he is likely quoting an early hymn of the church, we catch a further glimpse of what it cost for Jesus to be born among us. The clue is in verse 7, where we are told 'he emptied himself'. The root word in Greek is *kenosis*, which speaks of self-emptying, of giving up what you have. Jesus, being equal with God, or being one in the form of God, empties himself. Paul uses another expression to capture something of this when he writes, 'For you know the generous act of our Lord Jesus Christ, that though he was rich, yet for your sakes he became poor, so that by his poverty you might become rich' (2 Corinthians 8:9).

It's clear that this is not something that is done to Jesus or a fate that has overtaken him. This is his free-will offering – to void himself of that which constitutes his likeness to or his equality with God. As a result, he takes the form of a servant, to serve the will of the Father but also to serve those he came to live among. Being confronted with such a towering example of sacrifice, we can sense the challenge of 'how then shall we live?' And that is exactly the question we should ask, for it is for ethical reasons – 'Let the same mind be in you that was in Christ Jesus' (v. 5) – that Paul has spoken of this self-emptying.

On that Christmas morning, then, as Mary and Joseph looked upon the Christ child, what they saw was not Jesus in all his divine glory, but Jesus who had divested himself of all that spoke of his divinity and who had taken on our humanity. John Calvin, the great reformer, said that 'the humility of the flesh covers the divine majesty'. Charles Wesley's carol 'Hark! The Herald Angels Sing' contains the words:

Veiled in flesh the Godhead see!
Hail the incarnate Deity!
Pleased as man with man to dwell,
Jesus, our Emmanuel.

What can we learn from this? First and foremost, we learn that God loves each of us very deeply. This is simple to say, but hugely important. The Father's love (John 3:16) sends the Son (John 20:21) by the power of the Holy Spirit (Luke 1:35) – the Trinity is together in this salvation drama. For this reason, reciprocating God's love to us by expressing our devotion to him is our calling in life. Often, and understandably, we couch the claims of the gospel in terms of our need of forgiveness, and we do need that. Likewise we can speak of the gospel as a matter of justice, and that is a clear theme in scripture too. But there is another dimension, which is that the gospel calls and enables us to relate to God in ways that acknowledge the love he has shown towards us. I could say we need to express gratitude, but that word isn't strong enough. It's a reciprocal response of our love, freely given, that the gospel cries out for. The absence of such love – from God's perspective, an unrequited love – is achingly painful. The expression of such love is a most beautiful thing.

But there is something else here too. It's not just that God loves us but that we should love others. If God sees us of such worth, which isn't a surprise when we recall that we are made in his image, then this must shape the way we look upon others. When asked which was the greatest commandment, Jesus replied, 'Love the Lord your God' and 'Love your neighbour as yourself' (Mark 12:30–31, NIV). At its most obvious this is a call to deep respect and compassion, to see a need and meet it. It's a call to be charitable with our attitudes as well as with our time and money. Sadly, so much of modern life is structured to prevent this being a natural thing. We have rich and poor, and for the poor to become richer the rich need to become poorer; let's not pretend that's an appealing thought to most people, even though it's what this passage is about. We have class, political and ethnic divisions to such an extent that some argue against overseas aid because our priority should be 'our own', and others argue against helping even 'our own' because they don't deserve it. Compassion needs to find tangible expression – and not just in handouts, but by addressing the root causes of why some are poor, homeless or without access to health, education and jobs. This all flows from the incarnation.

Lastly, love God and love others, but also love self. Far from being an invitation to be a narcissist, this is a call to value who you are, a child of God made in his image. 'Love your neighbour *as yourself*' (Mark 12:31, my emphasis). In an age when the pressure to look like this or to achieve that or to own something else is a major force in our lives, we need to be quietly sure of *who* we are and *whose* we are. We need to accept ourselves just as we should accept others, with flaws and foibles but nonetheless as those created by God and loved by God.

25 December

The birth

Read LUKE 2:1–15

While they were there, the time came for her to deliver her child. And she gave birth to her firstborn son and wrapped him in bands of cloth, and laid him in a manger, because there was no place for them in the inn.

vv. 6–7

There's nothing quite like a birth! We can be sure that Joseph's and Mary's families wished them well when they set off from Nazareth, some perhaps glad that they were taking with them the unlikely story of a virgin birth. Along the way, strangers would have wished them well, and upon their arrival in Bethlehem it appears that so many were in town that there were no rooms immediately available. There may have been rooms elsewhere, but you can imagine that Mary just wanted to stop. Perhaps the offer of a place out back where the animals spent the night was seen as a kindness; millions of people today sleep in the same room as their animals in parts of the world where this is the norm.

The angels had been out in force already, so the shepherds would likely arrive soon, though Mary and Joseph weren't to know that. It's almost certain that a local birth attendant would have assisted in the birth, not least to reassure these first-time parents that all was well, to deliver the baby, to cut the cord and deliver the placenta, and to help the baby to the breast and say, 'I'll go now but I'll be back in a while, but I have a family to feed myself.' None of this is mentioned in Luke's gospel, and why would it be? It would have been assumed by his readers, and frankly these were not considered important details.

Besides, this is getting all gory and messy; let's get back to theology. Or perhaps not. For once, let's not disinfect the nativity with our usual dose of religious Domestos – the kind that kills 99% of all known authenticities, so that it's not just no room for Mary at the inn, but no room for any mention of flesh and blood. This is storytelling that eradicates the humanity of what happened and dresses it up in religious overtones beloved of a thousand paintings, resplendent with cherubs and heavenly haloes; Mary with a light blue, beautifully laundered outer garment; a neat semi-circle of sheep, goats and calves (cute ones only); and a perfectly located window allowing us to see a starlit sky beyond, neatly ignoring the fact that on a cold winter's night in Bethlehem the shutters would be closed – glass wouldn't be used in windows for another thousand years!

My point is this. Out of a well-intentioned desire to be reverential and to elevate the religious significance of God becoming incarnate, we have often created distance between Jesus and those we think should not get too close to him. The apostles tried to keep the children away; the Pharisees tried to keep the sinners away. As the church developed, the men kept the women away and the architecture kept the peasants away. The literates kept the illiterates away, and the priests kept the laity away. Christianity became respectable and that keeps the unrespectable away. But it is for the excluded ones that Jesus came. It is because of the mess that he came among us.

Christmas Day is the big day, of course, and we have sanctified versions of that too, with perfect families gathered round a perfect tree. But for most, it won't be perfect. For most it will be okay, but for some it won't even be that. The disappointments of the last year will nag away in the background, the dull pain that this should be the happiest of days but isn't. Some of us will be struggling with parents who have dementia and who have been reduced to a shadow of their former selves; we know it's not their fault but – being human – we sometimes come close to resenting them and their condition. There will be some who are lonely and others who are bereaved, and the absence of a loved one will be acutely painful. There will be worries about money and whether we spent too much trying to please everyone; about whether there will be a row when we get together; about whether someone will drink too much and embarrass themselves.

If your day is better than this, and I hope it will be, then give thanks to God for all that he has blessed you with. But if any part of this is your experience, then know that God understands and loves you. You're not second-best because your life isn't perfect or because your life is raw and broken and you're exhausted from putting up a good show. When you're frazzled and close to tears, and feeling like you've failed for whatever reason, God understands and loves you.

Whatever your circumstances, have a peaceful, and blessed, Christmas.

26 December

A dose of reality

Read LUKE 2:22–38

> **Now there was a man in Jerusalem whose name was Simeon; this man was righteous and devout, looking forward to the consolation of Israel, and the Holy Spirit rested on him. It had been revealed to him by the Holy Spirit that he would not see death before he had seen the Lord's Messiah.**
>
> vv. 25–26

The birth of a child is a time of great joy for the baby's parents, for the wider family and for friends. There are exceptions, of course – post-natal depression can make the experience less than easy, and the birth can reveal disabilities in the child that were not previously detected and which require time to adjust to. But even then, the future lies ahead like an open book, pages blank, ready for the story of this new life to be gradually written.

When Mary and Joseph came to the temple to present Jesus before the Lord, they were no doubt full of gratitude. But in encountering Simeon and Anna, they were given a new insight into the significance of this child's birth. Once again, we see a complex web of events coming together according to God's purposes.

Simeon, we are told, was a devout man, one to whom God had revealed that he would see 'the Lord's Messiah' in his lifetime. He was 'guided by the Spirit' (v. 27), though it is not clear whether that means he was guided to come to the temple that day or guided to recognise the child; the latter seems more likely. Simeon took Jesus in his arms and expressed praise that he could now die in peace, 'for my eyes have seen your salvation' (v. 30). Joseph and Mary were amazed at what was said about their child (v. 33), but Simeon's blessing included a warning to Mary – 'a sword will pierce your own soul too' (v. 35).

Present at the same time was Anna, who lived in the temple precincts. She approached the family as Simeon was speaking and she too praised God and 'began to speak about the child to all who were looking for the redemption of Jerusalem' (v. 38). Whether her audience was wider than the immediate family group, we can't be sure, but the timing of her words following on from Simeon's warning of pain to come would have provided some reassurance to Mary and Joseph. Surely the declarations made that day were added to those about which it is written, 'Mary treasured all these words and pondered them in her heart' (Luke 2:19; see also Luke 2:51).

Simeon's words that he could now depart in peace remind us that the peace of God is to be enjoyed even when everything in the garden isn't rosy. Simeon might have dreamt of a day when the glory of Israel would be restored, when people flocked to the temple to worship God, and when the Roman occupiers were gone. None of that looked even remotely close to happening, yet in the Christ-child he had seen the promise of God that this would come to pass, and that was enough for him.

We too live in a season of unfulfilled promises. We can lament the outgoing tide of faith in Jesus that we see in our own country, maybe in our own family too. But like Simeon, our hope is to be found in Christ, in seeing him as the same promise-fulfilment today as he was the day he was brought to the temple. Simeon knew in his spirit that God had acted decisively, and while all had not yet come to pass, Simeon's confidence was in God.

We might note also that peace is not always attainable without the pain of a pierced heart. Sometimes a solution emerges to life's problems, but it won't be able to nullify the pain we have already experienced. Anna's contribution was to encourage Mary and Joseph in all of this, and begin to declare the truth to a wider audience. Maybe she was the first evangelist.

Let's bring this closer to home. I don't think I've known a single person who hasn't had their share of pain to bear. Disappointments come from a multitude of sources, and at times they can threaten to overwhelm us. They can make us hard of heart, even cynical, uncertain who to trust anymore. Not just that, but we can allow our trust in God to weaken, for while we know that God is not one to reach down and overturn every example of human sin, wanton negligence or natural disaster, somewhere deep inside we are angry that God has allowed things to happen that bring us pain.

We have seen from the beginning that the peace Jesus offered his disciples was rooted in the knowledge of the presence of God. When we believe and trust that God is with us, then even if the situation cannot be resolved here and now, we can gain strength to endure, to persevere and to believe that the salvation of God, even for our own life, is in hand. This is what we learn from Simeon and Anna. In a small helpless infant, held in the arms of a poor and humble couple, they saw that God had acted decisively.

How that applies to your life, you must discover. Whatever you face today, tomorrow or in the years to come, know that God has acted and that one day, 'He will wipe every tear from their eyes. There will be no more death or mourning or crying or pain, for the old order of things has passed away' (Revelation 21:4, NIV).

That's the best I can offer you.

No, read that again. That really is *the best*, and I *can* offer it to you.

Part IV

Putting theory into practice

27 December

Blessed are the peacemakers

MATTHEW 5:9

> Blessed are the peacemakers, for they will be called children of God.

I was listening to *Desert Island Discs* a little while ago and Judy Murray, mother of tennis player Andy Murray, was the guest 'castaway'. One of her song choices was a Bay City Rollers number from the 1970s, when the band were at the height of their fame. Judy confessed that she had all the fan gear – the posters, the shortened jeans fringed in tartan and, of course, the tartan scarf. It's quite an image, but when we were young many of us dressed like our heroes, be they pop stars or sports champions. To do so conveys a sense of vicarious identity, a sense of pride or a feeling of belonging to a wider group of followers.

The call to be followers of Jesus, to emulate him and not just be admiring onlookers, is richly attested in scripture. Jesus called many to follow him. He said to his disciples, 'If you love me, keep my commands' (John 14:15, NIV), an indication that following him had certain expectations about how they were to live. He promised hardship, not just joy, when he said, 'Whoever does not carry the cross and follow me cannot be my disciple' (Luke 14:27). And he said, 'Let your light shine before others, so that they may see your good works and give glory to your Father in heaven' (Matthew 5:16), a sure indication that we are expected to be active in our discipleship.

In this context, the sermon on the mount (Matthew 5—7) has rightly been called a manifesto for the kingdom of God. If ever the question is asked, 'How shall we then live?', a large part of the answer is to be found here. And in the midst of the beatitudes is this pithy saying: 'Blessed are the peacemakers, for they will be called children of God.'

We have spoken of the presence of God as the source of the peace Jesus spoke about to his disciples, the peace that surpasses all understanding. But the presence of God is a multi-faceted idea. It is personal, for sure. I know personally that the birth of Christ inaugurated a new era in our relationship with God. That is not to say God was not with his people before the birth of Christ. But in Christ, God took our humanity into himself, atoned for our sinfulness and opened the way back to a full relationship with himself, to adoption as his sons and daughters and citizens of heaven. To heed this, to live in the light of this, is to be like a wise man who builds on rock rather than on sand (Matthew 7:24–27).

But the implications are wider than the personal; they address the world we live in. God's aim is to inaugurate his kingdom here on earth, as a foretaste of the kingdom to come. Even a cursory glance will see the centrality of the kingdom for the life and ministry of Jesus – the kingdom is mentioned 120 times in the gospels alone. Jesus said the kingdom was near (Matthew 10:7); he healed the sick as a sign of the kingdom (Matthew 4:23); he said humility was a condition of entering the kingdom (Matthew 18:4), that a child-like attitude was required (Matthew 19:14) and that riches were a stumbling block to entry (Matthew 19:23); and he told the poor that the kingdom of God belonged to them (Luke 6:20).

Time and again, it is God's kingdom that is in view, and being peacemakers is a clear obligation on those who are his followers, those who are citizens of this heavenly kingdom. The apostle Paul, writing to the church in Rome says, 'For the kingdom of God is not food and drink but righteousness and peace and joy in the Holy Spirit… Let us then pursue what makes for peace and for mutual edification' (Romans 14:17, 19). While this was written in the context of division about appropriate foods to eat, the principle is clear – peace is an integral characteristic of God's kingdom.

Earlier we saw how intensely practical this peace is, the shalom of God. It governs not just our relationship with God but the availability of those things that enable us to live a life of fullness – including food and water, a healthy environment and fairness for all. But to achieve these things requires action, not just sitting back and hoping for the best, or even hoping for the return of Jesus to make all things well. No, we are expected to be peace*makers* not peace-*waiters*, to be men and women who actively pursue a shalom agenda.

Shane Claibourne, in his book *Common Prayer: A liturgy for ordinary radicals*, writes:

> Peace is not just about the absence of conflict; it's also about the presence of justice... A counterfeit peace exists when people are pacified or distracted or so beat up and tired of fighting that all seems calm. But true peace does not exist until there is justice, restoration, forgiveness... Peacemaking doesn't mean passivity. It is the act of interrupting injustice without mirroring injustice, the act of disarming evil without destroying the evildoer, the act of finding a third way that is neither fight nor flight but the careful, arduous pursuit of reconciliation and justice. It is about a revolution of love that is big enough to set both the oppressed and the oppressors free.[4]

At the very least this reminds us that peacemaking is likely to be a full-time occupation! But notice carefully the link to justice – peace and justice are inextricably linked, a theme we will return to soon.

28 December

Peace and personal discipleship

Read GALATIANS 5:16–26

The fruit of the Spirit is love, joy, peace, patience, kindness, generosity, faithfulness, gentleness, and self-control.
vv. 22–23

Authenticity is in high demand these days. In an era of spin, the public are turned off by people who say one thing but live a different way. Don't be all glitzy on the front page if you're violent towards your partner in your private life. Don't Photoshop images of imperfect people to make them look perfect, and thereby set unattainable standards for vulnerable young people. Don't claim your car's emissions are as pure as the driven snow if in reality they are belching out filthy pollutants. It's all about being authentic, real or simply true. Not that this is new – Jesus was never slow to lambast those he knew to be hypocrites.

If we wish to say that peacemaking is part of who we are as Christ's disciples then our lives must bear witness to this. We must practise what we hope to preach, not only for our own well-being and not just to avoid a charge of hypocrisy, but so that our witness to Jesus, the Prince of Peace, will be authentic enough to be believed. Before we can realistically be peacemakers for others, we need to look into our own lives to see if there are areas where there is no peace, examine the root cause of that and then take action to address the gap. Let me suggest some areas that contribute to, or detract from, the presence of peace in our lives.

First, there is our relationship with God. We have to be at peace with God if we are to truly live a life of peace. Of course, those who avowedly shut God out of their life, or even deny that God exists, may still experience a measure of peace, especially if life pans out well for them. In fact, they may well say their lives are perfect! We shouldn't want to necessarily detract from that, but rather add to it, because *feeling* at peace and truly *being* at peace are different things. However good life is, it is better when God is known and worshipped. I hope that many of those who don't know God will find a warm embrace in his arms, as the prodigal son did in his father's (Luke 15:11–32) – and at that time I hope my reaction will be nothing like the elder brother's.

However, it is the Bible that dictates our approach, and Romans 5:1 is explicit in linking our relation to God to the objective reality of peace in our lives: 'Therefore, since we are justified by faith, we have peace with God through our Lord Jesus Christ.' Objectively, peace with God comes through faith in Jesus Christ. We shall see soon how our desire to be peacemakers will take us into the many realms of legitimate Christian concern for our world – from politics to environmental responsibility – but we must not shy away from the gospel message that Jesus is Lord and Saviour, and invite people to accept the claim he has upon their lives. If our faith in Christ brings us even a measure of peace, how can we withhold that from others?

Second, even for those of us who have made such a decision to follow Christ in the past, there is an ongoing work of character formation in order that our lives truly reflect the Lord we serve. Among the characteristics we should avoid are those listed in Galatians 5:19–21, and a rum lot they are too! But focus on the positive, and the nine traits listed in the verses that follow, Galatians 5:22–23.

Love heads the list, the greatest gift according to the apostle Paul in 1 Corinthians 13:13, and peace is mentioned as one of the nine, but it would be a mistake to separate these traits. Some commentators look to group them into three triplets, but frankly that structure doesn't work. I prefer to see these as behaviours and attitudes that stand or fall together as a single unit. A character being moulded to the likeness of Christ, while never perfect, will hopefully reveal each of these traits in generous measure. If it didn't, there would be work needed. So, without labouring the point, the presence of love in our hearts will be evidenced by a sense of joy, an aura of peace, a gentleness with people and so on. Similarly, peace will be evident because we view others with love; we do not allow present circumstances to rob us of joy; we are patient with people; we are kind, generous, gentle and known for self-control. To reverse this, if we lack self-control or have no love for people we will not be at peace, and so on.

Often, we look outside ourselves for reasons to explain our lack of peace. External influences do have a huge bearing on this – which is why over the next few days we will address some of these – but we must look first to our own lives, hearts and minds. That's where the root of our identity is, where we harbour all that is good and anything that isn't. It's in our hearts and minds that Christ needs to rule, the Spirit of God governing how we think and speak, how we respond and react.

This is why Paul says, 'And the peace of God, which surpasses all understanding, will guard your hearts and your minds in Christ Jesus' (Philippians 4:7).

29 December

Peace and the problem of suffering

Read ROMANS 8:18–30

I consider that the sufferings of this present time are not worth comparing with the glory about to be revealed to us.
v. 18

What's not to like about peace? Peace is like 'motherhood and apple pie', as our American friends would say. But if there is one issue that causes people to doubt or become suspicious about the peace of God, it's the problem of suffering. How do we reconcile the Bible's lofty promises with the brutal intrusion into everyday life of the sometimes horrific suffering many people have to endure, including those who have placed their trust in God?

Indeed, the storyline we are following is far from promising. From creation and fall and on through the story of God's people, we see a cry for peace from generation to generation. Even with the birth of Jesus, the Prince of Peace, there came suffering, as Herod slaughtered all boys aged under two years in and around Bethlehem (Matthew 2:16). Mary was promised that her heart would be broken; John the Baptist was later imprisoned and beheaded; and Jesus was tortured before being crucified. Stephen was martyred, and Peter, Paul and others were also executed for their faith. To this day, men and women die for their faith, often at the hands of sadistic tormentors. This promise of peace seems at best elusive and at worst just an illusion. Is it any wonder that over the years people have spoken of putting 'God in the dock' to answer the charge of being quiet, absent or uncaring in the face of suffering?

If we are to attempt a response, the first thing to say is that God in Christ came in the flesh precisely because of this suffering. Romans 8:18–30 draws our attention to the 'three groans' – the whole of creation groans (v. 22); we ourselves groan inwardly (v. 23); and in those moments when we cannot even pray because our faith is weak, the Holy Spirit intercedes for us with sighs, or groans, too deep for words (v. 26). All around us we see this groaning – 'man's inhumanity to man', natural disasters, catastrophic accidents, obscene terrorists and rogue viruses; all contribute to a daily diet of pain bordering on despair.

So before we cast a stone in God's direction, with the implied charge, 'Why don't you do something?', we must reckon with the fact that God has indeed done something. In the birth, life, death and resurrection of Jesus, God has irrevocably changed the landscape of human suffering forever. How it has changed we shall see in a moment, but it is at the cross that a fatal blow was dealt to the evil in this world that besets us. 'He himself bore our sins in his body on the cross' (1 Peter 2:24), and in so doing it appears that God has acted decisively to reset the personal moral imbalance that disturbs the world, like the spinning plates mentioned earlier.

How that relates to the 'groaning of creation' – the life-devouring earthquake, the electrical fault that triggers a fire in a tower block, or the outbreak of a deadly disease – I do not know for sure, but maybe acknowledging the moral and creational instability in the world allows us to hope for a day when the renewed earth of Revelation 21:1 will be a reality. Until then we live in this hurting world. It is still a world in which we can become more fully human; it gives us the joys as well as the dangers inherent in our daily lives. We take risks, because in doing so we grow both in knowledge and understanding of our world and of ourselves.

But risk mirrors tragedy, and tragedy hurts. It wouldn't hurt if we didn't love or care, but we do love and care, so we grieve and feel immeasurable pain. What is God to do? Our problem is that we cannot easily imagine another world, a world where there will be an end to suffering.

In the meantime we can choose to love and to be gentle, kind and compassionate. We can also choose to hate and to be violent, harsh and cold towards others. We can choose to sit at home and avoid the possibility of accidents, though we'd die of boredom and lose out on enjoying God's amazing world. If our choices are taken away, we do not create a world of peace; we create a world of robots, devoid of human beings. Our free will is what makes us human and makes our worship of God a true sacrifice of praise.

So far so bad. It sounds like I'm saying, 'Stop complaining. Life is good.' It isn't good – well, not always and not for everyone. But we haven't reckoned yet with the resurrection. The new world spoken of in the Bible, which we can't imagine, has already been glimpsed in the resurrection of Jesus. The apostle Paul says to the Corinthian Christians:

> In fact Christ has been raised from the dead, the first fruits of those who have died. For since death came through a human being, the resurrection of the dead has also come through a human being; for as all die in Adam, so all will be made alive in Christ.
>
> 1 CORINTHIANS 15:20–22

Some years ago, a young man, aged 18, in the church where I had been pastor went overseas for a year of mission. During that time abroad, he grew in faith from being someone for whom we had taken a risk to someone in whom God had done a mighty work. The church couldn't wait to receive him back. Imagine the feelings of his family and the church when news reached us that he had been killed in an accident on the way to the airport to fly home!

I anguished over this and eventually came to the conclusion that only the resurrection offered the consolation we craved. Even that understanding took a lot of time to come. Often, we want wrongs made right here and now but we have to weigh our lives in the scales of eternity.

A theology of heaven helps us realise that one day our sufferings will be reversed, just as Christ's death was reversed. That is the good news we preach. Yes, we will be ridiculed at times, for 'the message about the cross is foolishness to those who are perishing, but to us who are being saved it is the power of God' (1 Corinthians 1:18). But this is why Paul says, in today's passage, 'that the sufferings of this present time are not worth comparing with the glory about to be revealed to us' (v. 18).

That may be hard to believe, but that doesn't make it untrue.

30 December

Peace, justice and politics

Read ISAIAH 42:1–7

> Here is my servant, whom I uphold,
>   my chosen, in whom my soul delights;
> I have put my spirit upon him;
>   he will bring forth justice to the nations.
>   … to open the eyes that are blind,
> to bring out the prisoners from the dungeon,
>   from the prison those who sit in darkness.
>
> vv. 1, 7

The plaintive cry of a young child, 'It's not fair!', is all too common and reminds us that from our earliest years we have an innate sense of justice, and how important it is to be treated equitably. In fact, our whole lives depend on it. We expect a fair rate of pay for the work we do, and take for granted that we won't be arrested simply for driving down the road. When these things go awry, something deep inside is unsettled. Black youths who complain about the disproportionate number of times they are stopped in the street by police are reacting to a sense of injustice, as are those whose wages are capped while they see 'fat cats' walking away with millions. Justice is a deep-seated human conviction, because it is a reflection of God's own character. The psalmist writes, 'He loves righteousness and justice' (Psalm 33:5).

Peace and justice are inextricably connected. Justice is required for peace to thrive, and conversely there can be no justice without peace. On 17 December, we looked at the familiar verse, 'For a child has been born for us… and he is named… Prince of Peace' (Isaiah 9:6). The next verse is as follows:

His authority shall grow continually,
    and there shall be endless peace
for the throne of David and his kingdom.
    He will establish and uphold it
with justice and with righteousness
    from this time onwards and for evermore.
ISAIAH 9:7

So, the endless peace of this kingdom will be established with justice and righteousness. In which case, what does justice actually mean?

In Isaiah 42:1–7, we have the first of the four so-called servant songs, which speak of the Messiah to come. In this unmistakable prophecy, we are told that God delights in him (v. 1), that he is gentle in character and speech (vv. 2–3) and that 'he will not grow faint or be crushed until he has established *justice* in the earth' (v. 4, emphasis added). These verses are directly applied to Jesus in Matthew 12:15–21.

In these verses, therefore, the aim of the coming Messiah, the Prince of Peace, is to bring justice to the earth. Remember, without justice there can be no peace, so if peace is the goal, justice is the means. A few verses later, in a passage directed at the servant to come, justice is illustrated thus:

I have given you as a covenant to the people,
    a light to the nations,
    to open the eyes that are blind,
to bring out the prisoners from the dungeon,
    from the prison those who sit in darkness.
ISAIAH 42:6–7

Here we see the very practical nature of justice. Jesus, the Prince of Peace, will be a light to the nations, the one who will illumine the way home to a place of safety, exemplified when Jesus says of himself, 'I am the light of the world' (John 8:12). We are told that the

Messiah will bring justice by opening the eyes of the blind, words that can be taken both figuratively and literally.

Figuratively, blindness to God is used to speak of the need we have for an encounter with God. The apostle Paul uses the image this way when writing to the Jewish believers in Rome: 'if you call yourself a Jew… and if you are sure that you are a guide to the blind, a light to those who are in darkness… you, then, that teach others, will you not teach yourself?'(Romans 2:17–21). Clearly, he is talking about spiritual blindness. And before we slip into lazy stereotypes about those of other faiths being 'in darkness', we might consider that people of other faiths are arguably less blind than many in the secular west who profess no faith. And are we confident that even we who have come to faith are not blind ourselves? To the needs of our neighbours? To the priorities we pursue in life? Let us be slow to judge (Romans 2:1).

But of the many miracles Jesus did he also gave physical sight to the blind, a sign of the kingdom to come, where there would no longer be disease and death. Healing the sick is a justice issue, especially in a world where so many diseases can be cured for a few pence worth of childhood immunisation.

To bring out prisoners from darkness has similar overtones. It can be interpreted literally, and in a world where in many countries prisoners are almost abandoned and the key thrown away, surviving in vile conditions, bringing hope even to those who are guilty in the eyes of the law echoes the mercy of a forgiving God. But imprisonment has another dimension, for poverty is the biggest limiter of freedom anywhere in the world. The psalmist is clear: 'I know that the Lord maintains the cause of the needy, and executes justice for the poor' (Psalm 140:12). Hundreds of millions of people today are imprisoned by circumstances out of their control. They are born poor and cannot escape poverty, for the cards are stacked against them. Meanwhile those of us who are better off are able to increase our wealth just because we have wealth to start with. The nourishing family life of my early childhood, along with an excellent education, meant that I could get a good job and, in time, buy a house, which in turn has increased in value many times more than I paid for it. People in poverty often struggle educationally, and so their children do likewise. At the extreme, millions of children give up school because they need to work to support their family, and the cycle of poverty continues.

Are these gospel issues? Yes they are! They are gospel issues because they are kingdom issues, because they relate to human flourishing – education as a route out of poverty; medical care as a doorway to well-being; jobs and roles as a celebration of our God-given abilities. Even in our care and support for the elderly, the sick or the disabled, our goal is that everyone lives with dignity and is not measured according to some indicator of economic worth.

The gospel of peace, the promotion of justice and the politics that shape our world – all are interwoven and all are bound up with living our faith as Christians.

31 December

Peace, creation care and the poor

Read PSALM 104:10–23

> You cause the grass to grow for the cattle,
>   and plants for people to use,
> to bring forth food from the earth,
>   and wine to gladden the human heart,
> oil to make the face shine,
>   and bread to strengthen the human heart.
>
> vv. 14–15

Over the years I've visited some wonderful places, and a global conference in Hawaii was as special as you might think. As we flew across thousands of miles of ocean, finally to pick out a few specks that are the Hawaiian islands, we quickly became aware of how intertwined the links are between the people and their environment. We were greeted on the opening evening by local Christians with a traditional chant used for generations to welcome people to this beautiful place:

> We are an island community in the middle of the vast Pacific Ocean. Because of this we are sensitive to the winds that blow around us, to the waves that crash upon our shores, to the rains that fall to nurture our precious lands. We are dependent on one another to survive. All that comes from our great God is precious to us.

As our global atmosphere has warmed over recent years, the implications for all who live on this small planet are becoming very real. Some years ago, as Christians began to connect caring for creation with their faith, and even talked about it as part of the mission of the church, I was sceptical. I didn't doubt either the science behind global warming or its impact but I couldn't see the connection to the gospel. I was blind; today I'm almost embarrassed at how slow I was to get it.

The person whose work helped me most is Stella Simiyu, a botanist and member of the council of A Rocha, the international Christian conservation charity. She posed the question, 'Can you imagine your life without your shops and supermarkets, your petrol station or your pharmacy?' It didn't take long for me to realise the huge impact that would make on *my* life. She continued, 'The rural poor depend directly on the natural resource base [of seas, rivers and forests]. This is where their pharmacy is, this is where their supermarket is, this is in fact their fuel station, their power company, their water company.'[5]

If we can make the connection between the gospel and the work of justice for the poor, it's just a small step further to think about creation care. The poor often live with a closer relationship to the land and the sea than the rich do, but it is the rich who have the greater impact on the health of the environment. We are seeing this more and more as global warming gives rise to droughts and floods, and even in areas of the developed world we now routinely see catastrophic weather events.

Go back to the understanding of shalom we explored on 3 December, and the physicality of the concept. Peace has as much to do with food and shelter, safety and security as it does our relationship with God. At the base of Maslow's hierarchy of needs is our physiological need of food, drink, clothing and shelter.[6] Sometimes we remove our faith from the physical and give it an altogether other-worldly dimension. Yes, it does have that, but it also has its feet planted firmly on the ground. Jesus responded to the question of which of the commandments was the greatest by saying:

> 'You shall love the Lord your God with all your heart, and with all your soul, and with all your mind, and with all your strength.'

> The second is this, 'You shall love your neighbour as yourself.'
> There is no other commandment greater than these.
> MARK 12:30–31

Note that final comment – there is *no commandment* greater than these. In Matthew's account of this conversation he ends by saying, 'On these two commandments hang all the law and the prophets' (Matthew 22:40). In different words we have this similarly stupendous claim that the whole of the Hebrew scriptures boils down to this – love God and love your neighbour.

These commandments are more than simply two separate priorities. They are inextricably linked; they stand or fall together. We cannot choose to love God but ignore our neighbour, for to do so is to ignore what it means to love God. The obvious support to this is Matthew 25:31–46, where Jesus says, 'I was hungry and you gave me food, I was thirsty and you gave me something to drink, I was a stranger and you welcomed me, I was naked and you gave me clothing, I was sick and you took care of me, I was in prison and you visited me' (vv. 35–36), and – in answer to the question 'When did we do all that?' – 'Just as you did it to one of the least of these who are members of my family, you did it to me' (v. 40). So, to love God is to love the poor, and if we have love for the poor (and ourselves) we will care for creation.

Love for the poor often triggers charitable impulses. But it isn't enough to simply deliver aid to those in need; we need to live and act in such a way that they won't need our aid. Hélder Câmara (1909–99) was a Brazilian Catholic archbishop who worked among the poor for most of his life. He is quoted as saying, 'When I give food to the poor, they call me a saint. When I ask why they are poor, they call me a communist.' We too have to go beyond asking how we can help the poor to ask, 'Why are they poor? Why are there no jobs, no schools and no vaccinations? Why are there floods, droughts and famines in the first place?' In some cases the cause is corruption or war, and even in recent years the west has rushed into conflicts where other courses should have been taken. But often it is our lifestyle and our voracious globalised economy that are ravaging the natural resources that the poor need for daily living. Our constant desire to have larger economies drives climate change. Carbon emissions have poisoned our atmosphere, and as ice caps melt and sea levels rise, hundreds of millions of the world's poorest are in danger. Sadly, the worst of climate change will likely be experienced by our children and grandchildren, and far worse by the children and grandchildren of today's poor.

We cannot deny it is a depressing outlook. But hopefully it is not too late. Gradually nations are making changes, and the UK aspires to be a leader among nations aiming for a low-carbon economy.[7] I love the sight of wind turbines, not just because I find them aesthetically more pleasing than the pylons that populate our landscape (though there are fans of those too!) but because each one is a sign that we are serious about harnessing renewable energy. We must keep the pressure on in this area for this is the greatest hope we have for mitigating the climate damage we have done. The UK's overseas aid budget is at least respectable and has been maintained through difficult years. Here too we must keep the pressure on politicians to maintain that commitment or, even better, to do more. Locally, how we live and use our wealth (and give away our wealth) are indicators of how much we see the connection between loving God, loving our neighbour, peace and justice, creation care and our responsibility towards the poor.

1 January

Peace, politics
and our interconnected world

Read ROMANS 13:1–7

> For the same reason you also pay taxes, for the authorities
> are God's servants, busy with this very thing. Pay to all what
> is due them – taxes to whom taxes are due, revenue to whom
> revenue is due, respect to whom respect is due, honour to
> whom honour is due.
>
> vv. 6–7

How many times have you heard politicians say that Christians
should keep their noses out of politics? It's usually said when
criticisms are striking close to home or when shortcomings in a
party's policies are under the spotlight.

We've seen already that God's heart is to restore shalom, but what
if we agreed that the goal of politics was to do the same? Many
politicians, to listen to their speeches, seem to think the goal is to
create wealth and prosperity. While that might be a part of it, the
ultimate goal should be to create shalom, not to create people who
are rich but stressed or unhappy, or people who have become rich by
plundering from others or from God's creation.

The Bible is full of godly people involved in politics. Joseph was used
by God in a position of authority over all of Egypt (Genesis 41:41);
Daniel became the third-highest ranking person in the kingdom
(Daniel 5:29); Esther saved her people because of her privileged
position (Esther 8:5); and Nehemiah was able to lead the rebuilding
of the walls of Jerusalem because of his connections to the king

(Nehemiah 2:4–6). In the New Testament, less is said about key individuals, for the focus is now on the life of Jesus and the early church, but it is clear from today's passage that there is a place for governing authorities, because their authority also comes from God.

I don't advocate for Christians to vote for a particular political party – red, blue, yellow, green or whatever. Such a suggestion would be absurd. We all have to decide for ourselves, and that will most likely involve making some compromises. But one thing we can't do is absent ourselves from the world of politics. Our faith compels us to be involved, because *politics*, in the meaning of the root Greek word, is simply the affairs of the city. As we have seen, if there is one thing God is concerned about it's the affairs of the city – the nations and the peoples of the world. And his goal is peace.

Nowhere is peacemaking more relevant than in international relations. In recent years the violent oppression of dissenting voices (e.g. in Egypt and Syria) and of minorities (e.g. the Kurdish Yazidis or the Rohingya Muslims of Burma), and the outbreak of war between nations (too often armed and backed by the west) have been all too frequent. I am not a pacifist; I don't believe that it is always wrong to fight. Many Christians and others *are* pacifists and should be listened to, but I am not arguing that position here. Rather my point is that war is always a disaster, is always a failure, always wreaks havoc in the lives of innocent people and is always to be avoided if humanly possible. For these reasons, Christians committed to being peacemakers should ensure, at the very minimum, that war is only ever the last resort, and even then that it is undertaken only with appropriate means and in such a way as to minimise the loss of life.

But peace, as we have seen, means far more than the absence of war. We must, therefore, encourage Christians to be involved, as people of faith, in the decision-making processes that affect our nation. This is not because people of faith have a monopoly on virtue, common sense or the necessary skills; rather because Christians can and do have important things to contribute from their particular faith tradition on many national and international issues. As followers of the one who came to serve not to be served, we can shape the national conversation in such a way that the human propensity to look after self alone is tempered by our responsibility to care for others, especially in regard to social welfare and our treatment of refugees and asylum seekers. As recipients of God's free gift of grace, we can point out that to be a generous nation that is quick to respond to all manner of international disasters is to our credit. (Again, to be clear, this is not to say that generosity is a characteristic unique to Christians.) As those who seek God's kingdom, an effective way we can make his rule evident is through the regulation of national and international economies, attending to issues such as job creation, fair wages, safe working conditions, affordable housing and environmental protection.

At the international level, we should attend to religious liberty as part of our commitment to fundamental human rights. All over the world we see Christians persecuted, and in these situations we may be the only voice they have to speak out against the oppression they suffer. But if our commitment means anything we must also stand by those of other faiths. Sadly there are all too many cases of Muslims persecuting Christians, but Christians are not alone in suffering for their faith, as seen in the recent examples of the Muslim Rohingya in Burma and Ahmadi in Pakistan and elsewhere.

Christians, therefore, should be encouraged to be politically engaged – participating in political parties as members, writing to their MPs and joining in. But, I stress, the aim is for a kingdom of godly peace and justice to be brought to bear and not the promotion of one party over another. It wouldn't be difficult to argue from the political left or right the wisdom of taking their route to success, however that is defined. What isn't acceptable is to disengage, to say this has nothing to do with my faith. It has everything to do with our faith! Jesus came into our human experience to redeem our world and its people. Politics is a key part of that redemptive process.

2 January

Peace, gender, race and rank

Read GALATIANS 3:23-29

> There is no longer Jew or Greek, there is no longer slave or
> free, there is no longer male and female; for all of you are one
> in Christ Jesus.
>
> v. 28

Last time I looked there were still Jewish and Greek people, there
were still (despite slavery being illegal) slaves, and there sure were
women and men walking round the streets. So what did Paul mean
by 'there is no longer'?

While over the centuries the church has been guilty of racial
prejudice, condoning slavery and the subjugation of women, the
gospel has no place for such things. For all its failings, the church
at its best champions the dignity of everyone – no favouritism, no
second-class citizens, no people of less worth than others. It would
not be difficult even today to find evidence where we fall short in
these areas, but to stand for these things, to speak out and act, is
our work as disciples. Why? Because they represent the heart of God
before whom, one day, when the biblical vision of shalom is fulfilled,
people from every tribe and language will stand as one and praise
him (Revelation 7:9). There will be no VIPs, no business and economy
class, no caste system and no foreigner.

That's the vision, but what about the reality? Human history is
beset with violence – physical, emotional, psychological and
spiritual – against those perceived as different. That violence has
been manifested in prejudice, persecution, exploitation, hatred,
abuse, homophobia, misogyny and xenophobia. It doesn't make for

pretty reading and still less for pretty living. Recognising this and addressing it is a key issue if we want men and women to experience peace.

For inspiration, of course, we have the ministry of Jesus, which was characterised by his radical inclusion of all whom others would exclude or alienate. With women, his relationships were extraordinary for their time. He healed a woman on the Sabbath and, in the face of opposition from religious leaders, he called her 'a daughter of Abraham' (Luke 13:16), an honorific title that put her on a par with Jewish men, who were often referred to as sons of Abraham. He speaks to a Samaritan woman and she becomes a witness to Christ, leading others to faith in him (John 4:1–42). He saves a woman from stoning (John 8:3–11), pointing out that those who judged her were themselves sinners. Jesus had women among his disciples, as evidenced by verses such as Matthew 12:49: 'And pointing to his disciples, he said, "Here are my mother and my brothers."' Mary and Martha were among Jesus' closest followers, and they not only were taught by him but ministered to him. Other women supported him financially (Luke 8:2–3).

Two examples stand out. First, Jesus' mother, Mary, was honoured among women of all time, as she bore the Son of God in her womb, helped him develop to adulthood and bore the pain of his crucifixion. Sadly, Mary's role has at times been caught in disputes between diverging church traditions, but she has a place of pre-eminence for her role in the salvation story. Second, as attested to by all the gospels, the first witnesses to the resurrection of Jesus are women. The witness of the early church was built on their testimony, and in women like Priscilla (Acts 18:26) and Junia, or Junias (Romans 16:7), who is named as 'prominent among the apostles', we have no reasons to see women as other than equal co-workers for the gospel. Therefore, it is part of our mandate beyond the church that we should do all we can to address the injustices of sexism that are so prevalent in our society.

The same can be said of racism and xenophobia. These are alive and well today, as evidenced by the language used of refugees ('they are coming in swarms'), the animosity shown towards Muslims, and the continuing experience of injustice by black and ethnic minority communities. These are also gospel issues – and just as relevant to us when they occur in other countries. In contrast, in Jesus we see one who honoured and accepted Samaritans (John 4), even, contrary to the commonly held views of the time, portraying them as the good guys (Luke 10:33). Likewise, we should be engaged wherever we see minorities treated with prejudice in any way.

It's one thing to be a protester on these issues; it's another to be a living example. Our churches can be just that – the embodiment of a way of living in community where there is no unjust differentiation between Jew or Greek, slave or free, male or female. With so many of our churches now becoming communities of people from different nations, we should ensure that this diversity is included in worship and in leadership. Men and women should be visible in leadership too, with these different voices contributing to a true expression of a multi-voiced church.

How is this relevant to peacemaking? When Paul wrote to the Ephesians he couched the gospel in terms of breaking down barriers between Jews and Gentiles:

> For he is our peace; in his flesh he has made both groups into one and has broken down the dividing wall, that is, the hostility between us... that he might create in himself one new humanity in place of the two, thus making peace... So then you are no longer strangers and aliens, but you are citizens with the saints and also members of the household of God.
> EPHESIANS 2:14–15, 19

Peacemaking demands that we remove all barriers between us.

3 January

Peace and the body of Christ

Read ROMANS 12:9–21

If it is possible, so far as it depends on you, live peaceably with all.
v. 18

Given that sometimes we have conflict in our own homes, it should come as no surprise that conflict can also arise in church. We're human, so conflict will happen, and sometimes the result can even be beneficial. Therefore, the issue is not how to avoid conflict per se, but how to avoid unnecessary conflict and how to handle conflict when it arises, because how we do so will enhance or damage our claim to be a community of peace-builders.

At the personal level the Bible contains good advice. For example: 'If another member of the church sins against you, go and point out the fault when the two of you are alone', followed by the suggestion that if that doesn't work take others with you and if that still doesn't work bring it to the attention of the church (Matthew 18:15–17). But before you go charging off I would also suggest we ask ourselves, 'Is this worth the effort?' In any community we will encounter people with attitudes and behaviours that are different from our own, and it's part of life to accept such differences. Someone may disagree with us, and they may even be wrong, but is that always such a big deal?

If there really is an issue, then it is better addressed than left to fester. Again, ask yourself, 'How would you react if someone came to you to raise a concern about something you said or did that caused offence? What would make it easier for you to hear in such a way that you react well?' It's no small matter to confront someone, and how that person reacts is vital. I'd like to think that if someone came to me, they wouldn't be shown the door, but I'd at least be willing to listen. Remember, communication is not what's said, it's what's heard, so choose your timing, approach and words well.

A word of advice I want to give at this point is very sensitive, so I'll try to say this carefully. My experience over many years in church life is that *some* older people think they can say outrageous things and that it will go unchallenged. On a few occasions I've had to say to people, 'You just can't say that!' Please understand I'm not applying this to all older people, but old age sometimes seems to cause people to lose their inhibitions, and I've known real offence to be caused as a result. On the positive side, older people have a hugely influential role as encouragers of younger generations. One word from a respected elder in the church can be liberating. If you're older, be known as an encourager. If you're younger, talk to your elders and you'll often be blessed with their wisdom.

Let's throw the net wider and into deeper waters – what about conflict in the broader church? Sadly, we've seen disputes in recent years about vital issues like women in ministry and homosexuality, as the church adapts to a world where some inherited beliefs and assumptions are challenged. People can feel they are defending the very gospel itself –that the 'word of God' is at stake. Whenever I hear a phrase like 'the Bible is clear about this', I groan inwardly, because usually it's obvious that the Bible isn't as clear as we might think and it certainly isn't clear to everyone. Let me offer a few signposts, recognising there isn't space for more.

First, pause and ask whether all issues are of equal importance. I would be quick to rush to the barricades if, for instance, there was a growing view that Jesus was just a good man or that the resurrection didn't really happen. Why? Because for me the core of our faith is the person and work of Christ; everything else comes second – and a distant second too. We live like this anyway – on a typical Good Friday, towns up and down the country have a march of witness that brings together Methodists, Baptists, Anglicans, Catholics and other denominations, united in our devotion and witness to Christ as Lord and Saviour. In times long gone, we burned each other at the stake! We have different views about baptism, communion, ministry, church membership, scripture and so on, yet what unites us is Christ. Sometimes we need that perspective within the local church, not just between church traditions.

Second, to draw a lesson from my own Baptist tradition (with our early experience of persecution at the hand of established church authorities), freedom of dissent and liberty of conscience go hand-in-hand. So, in relation to issues we may disagree over, we recognise that unity is more important than uniformity. In fact, I'd go so far as to say that our unity is enhanced when our lack of uniformity is recognised but we still love and remain in fellowship with each other. The place of gay relationships in the church is today's hot-button issue. There will not be universal agreement any time soon, but meanwhile the world looks on to see how the church treats today's 'outsiders', and gay people themselves have lives to live and in many cases a desire to follow Christ and be loved and accepted in the church. Outside of affirming churches, there is talk of seeking a 'pastoral accommodation' that mirrors the position taken towards divorced people. No theological modification has been made to marriage that creates space for divorce, yet many divorced people are able to remarry and remain in good standing in the church. This kind of solution must be found before the judgment of history declares that the church has again failed in its duty to love.[8]

The apostle Paul wrote to the Christians in Rome, 'If it is possible, so far as it depends on you, live peaceably with all' (Romans 12:18). While this was primarily about living among unbelievers, the principle applies everywhere. The double qualification – 'If it is possible, so far as it depends on you' – recognises the difficulty of achieving this, but if it is challenging then we should redouble our efforts to make it work. Unity is far, far more important than uniformity over secondary issues.

4 January

Peace in unexpected places

Read LUKE 10:1–11

> Whatever house you enter, first say, 'Peace to this house!' And if anyone is there who shares in peace, your peace will rest on that person; but if not, it will return to you.
>
> vv. 5–6

Just as the love and grace of God extends further than the boundaries of the church, so too men and women of peace can be found outside of the family of faith. Today, in many parts of the world, mission strategies are being built upon the approach seen in today's passage – finding people who may not be believers but whose hearts are inclined towards peace, then building upon their welcome or point of entry to create a community to share the good news of Jesus.

My own experience is striking. In Asia, where BMS has worked for many years, we have teams of national evangelists who will go to visit the elders of a village and ask if they can come with friends and spend time with the villagers. On receiving permission, they come and often spend an afternoon playing sports and games, and offer a short gospel talk afterwards. Religious discourse is a strong and natural part of many Asian societies, so this is rarely seen as strange or problematic. During the afternoon, and afterwards, conversations are held with those who participate or are simply there as onlookers, and the offer is made to come back and talk more. If someone agrees to host the returning visitors, then the invitation from that 'person of peace' becomes the next step in building a relationship with the village. In time, a Bible study group may start and many may come to faith. Interestingly, though the man or woman of peace is key to this process, they themselves may not come to faith. We long for them to do so, and they often do, but as ever these things are in God's hands.

Turning to your own community, ask yourself who the men and women of peace might be. They may be those well regarded by others or having a degree of influence, such as a head teacher or councillor. It may be a long-term resident in your street or simply someone in your friendship group. It could be someone at work or a mum at the toddler group that everyone gets on with, or the manager of a local cafe who welcomes those who – strange as it may seem to him or her – bring their Bible and study it while sipping an excellent cappuccino. Praying into those key relationships is a way of entering into the lives of others. The key as always is authenticity – to be genuinely interested in relationships with people whether or not they respond positively. Clearly if they do not respond favourably to conversations about spiritual things you need to respect that, but hoping to share our faith is a God-honouring endeavour, one that blesses countless people as they in turn come to know of God's love for them.

The language of 'persons of peace' may be a strange concept initially, but behind it is a recognition that there are good people everywhere who wish well for others and are willing to put themselves out to help. This should never come as a surprise to us, because everyone is created in the image of God. Recognising an inherently good and peaceable disposition in others is a reminder, if it was needed, that Christians do not have a monopoly on being good Samaritans – the good Samaritans have that! In fact, over many years I have seen wonderful examples of loving servanthood displayed by countless people of no faith and other faiths. It is to our detriment when we demarcate between church and non-church and assume that there is goodness only on one side of the equation. Such a stance is folly!

But what does it mean to speak of someone as a 'person of peace'? Does it mean that they have the peace of God that we've been speaking about? Not necessarily. But our approach is intended to bring a blessing to that place, to bring a message of peace that echoes their peaceable welcome to us. That should always be our primary motivation, to go to others in the peace of Christ.

In today's passage, Jesus instructs the apostles that if their approach is welcomed they are to remain and accept hospitality but if it is rejected, they should wipe off the dust from their feet (v. 11). I'll be honest, this doesn't read comfortably at first glance, as it needs translating from its ancient context. In biblical times, hospitality was everything. Even today, Middle Eastern culture puts a very high premium on hospitality. Strangers or visitors will be welcomed into the bosom of the family and the table will be heavy-laden with food with the aim, it seems, that there is always more than people can actually eat. (That way you really know you've put enough before your guests.) But if hospitality was ever denied and a visitor deemed unwelcome, then you could indeed walk away in disgust. This cannot be translated literally into the different norms of today's western culture, though there are aspects of the warmth of hospitality we could learn from! We have limited expectation of asking for or receiving hospitality from strangers, but we know that to build a genuine relationship with someone takes time, and from that will flow whatever hospitality we can give and receive. This is not better or worse; it's just different. What is important in all cultures is that friendships are genuine. But the faith we have in Christ is in itself an example of God's hospitality, that he would welcome us when we were far off and prepare not just a feast but an experience of abundant life that will last for eternity.

May God give us the strength to go out to these unexpected places and share this priceless gift with those we meet.

5 January

Bow down and worship

Read MATTHEW 2:1–12

> On entering the house, they saw the child with Mary his mother; and they knelt down and paid him homage. Then, opening their treasure-chests, they offered him gifts of gold, frankincense, and myrrh.
>
> v. 11

As we approach the twelfth day of Christmas and the end of our studies, we prepare to celebrate the day when the three visitors from the east came following a star to find the one they said was to be the king of the Jews. In reality, their arrival may have come some time after the birth, suggested by the mention in verse 11 of 'the house' (not stable) where they found Mary and her 'child' (not baby).

I wonder what it was that made the Magi set out on their journey? Commentators largely agree that these three were not kings but priests from Persia, that is, the area that is now largely modern-day Iran. (How interesting that the gospel is reaping such a rich harvest among Iranians these days!) Like many of their priestly line, they studied the stars and were something akin to astrologers. As it happens, they also lived at a time when there was widespread expectation of the birth of a messiah. The Hebrew scriptures were the source for much of the expectation, but there were other sources too. The Roman poet Virgil, around 42BC, wrote a major work, called *Eclogues*, which featured the birth of a saviour who would become divine and rule the world. The meaning of the poem was much debated, but it fed into a general sense that maybe a saviour was to be born. In some ways this doesn't matter, other than to note that something triggered the Magi to set off on their quest; whether it was a juxtaposition of planets or the appearance of a comet that was interpreted as a sign that a birth of great significance was imminent, it's hard to say.

The point is that for people who search for God – or for meaning, or however the quest is described – each story is unique, but each story can lead to Christ if there are those who, like the Bethlehem star, guide the way. If the peace of God that surpasses all understanding is worth what we say it's worth, maybe our role is to be there as a companion on the journey. We often think our primary spiritual role, and a daunting one at that, is to be an evangelist, giving people a potted history of the gospel in a half-dozen pithy phrases. Sometimes that's exactly what's needed, but on other occasions our ministry may be to encourage a weary traveller to keep going and keep trusting and to reassure them that you are praying for them as they travel.

As the Magi approached the end of their journey, they would have been tired from months of travel. Sometimes we want our quests to be over quickly, especially in today's on-demand world. But some things take time, especially a pilgrimage, and God knows the value of allowing time for people to spend on their search. Tired travellers need inspiration, of course, and nothing will bring renewed energy more than the possible vision of what they'll see when they arrive.

The Magi would have been delighted and relieved to reach Jerusalem, and they soon started to ask questions about the newborn king's whereabouts. Their questions were picked up by spies or informers, and word came to Herod's ear. Shortly after they are sent to Bethlehem, charged with returning in due course so the evil Herod could go and worship the child too! After one more leg of their journey they arrived in Bethlehem, where we're told that the star had stopped, though that would hardly highlight the exact house. We can imagine that they asked around again, as they'd done in Jerusalem, and I wonder what it was they heard. Was there already news about this child that had spread because of the testimony of the shepherds concerning the appearance of angels? The shepherds were local men, and their testimony would have been the talk of the town. If Joseph and Mary had stayed there, with many knowing that a special child had been born, we can be sure that local people would have been protective of the family. After all, it was only five miles to Jerusalem, the ruling headquarters of the Roman occupiers.

On entering the house, the Magi, we are simply told, paid homage. They knelt down, opened their treasure chests and offered gifts of gold, frankincense and myrrh. Here was the end of the line for the Magi. It began with enquiring minds and a resolve to set out on a journey. The voyage had been arduous and prolonged and the Magi had needed words and signs to guide them along the way, but now they were here. And they knelt down. They knelt down before the child who was the only begotten Son of God, who was before time began and will be to all eternity, but who for now had become flesh.

The poverty of the surroundings didn't put them off, nor the simplicity of the family. We too should learn from that, for over the many generations that men, women and children have come to faith, they have bent the knee under the stars, as well as in humble chapels and the greatest of cathedrals. Simple folk, unschooled and impoverished, have bent the knee alongside scholars and saints, kings and queens.

The Prince of Peace had come.

As God had said and the prophets foretold, the Prince of Peace had come.

As Gabriel announced and Mary received, the Prince of Peace had come.

As the creation groaned and the people prayed, the Prince of Peace had come.

'And they knelt down and paid him homage.'

6 January

A personal word

NUMBERS 6:24–26

> The Lord bless you and keep you;
> The Lord make his face to shine upon you, and be gracious
>   to you;
> The Lord lift up his countenance upon you, and give you
>   peace.

Today we finish our exploration of God's peace, yet naturally there is so much more that could be said. But as we draw towards the close, I'd like you to mentally step aside from study mode and for a moment adopt a different pose. Imagine you've sat down in a comfortable armchair near to a large window, and the sun is beaming through. It's not a hot day, but it's one of those days when the heat of the sun is noticeable and welcome. The house is quiet, and this feels like 15 precious minutes to yourself. Enjoy them!

The Lord bless you.

God wants you to know that you are deeply loved by him; the kind of love that aches when you're away from the person you love; the kind of love that causes your heart to miss a beat when you see them again. To be blessed is to experience by faith what it means to be a child of God. To know his forgiveness and grace and acceptance. But it's also to have all that you need in life. It covers our food and drink, our security and protection – the things we sometimes take for granted, having disconnected them from any sense that it is by God's creation these things are provided.

Give thanks for these blessings.

The Lord keep you.

Whatever happens to you, whether life pans out as you hope or not, you are his by faith, forever. Nothing can take you from him. You are secure for all eternity. You are his created and adopted child, with an inheritance you can never lose.

Praise him for this extravagant gift.

The Lord make his face to shine upon you.

This is where the sun's rays can help, for you will know that the Bible says that God dwells in unapproachable light. You cannot go close to God, but God can make himself known to you. He has done that in Christ, the light of the world, and his face is orientated towards you. It's an image, of course, but a powerful one. God is on your side. He's in your corner. He's rooting for you, cheering for you, proud of you.

Take a moment to tell him what this feels like.

The Lord be gracious to you.

Ah yes, grace. Without it we're sunk. We've failed the test, fallen short of the mark, missed the target. But grace overlooks all this; or rather grace puts this right. Grace puts the winner's medal around your neck and garlands you with a crown of righteousness. How can that be? It's simple really. Jesus took your place and mine. Took what was coming our way. Soaked it up. Didn't even complain. And if he was gracious once, he will be gracious always. Where are you today?

Ask for a portion of grace to face the challenges set before you today.

The Lord lift up his countenance upon you.

Here we have an example of Hebrew parallelism, saying the same thing twice but using different words – like 'the earth is the Lord's, and everything in it, the world, and all who live in it' (Psalm 24:1, NIV). There is something of that here, but often there is some new disclosure because of the different words chosen. Here you are encouraged to see that on the face that is turned towards you, the expression – the countenance – is to be welcomed not feared. There is a smile on the face of God as he sees the very person you also see when you look in the mirror. But when you look in the mirror, you are likely a harsher judge than God. You look and wince; he looks and beams. You look and are ashamed; he looks and is proud. You look and wonder, 'What if?'; he looks and wonders, 'Why not!'

Take a moment to tell him how you feel.

The Lord give you peace, shalom.

God wants you to know the calm contentment of knowing all will be well. I can't say 'all *is* well' because you wouldn't believe me. You'd be rude to me, and you'd be right. To say all is well would be a mockery of the world and its people, those who struggle to survive and who have borne far more than their share of suffering, indignity, shame and disappointment. The knowledge of their presence leaves you and me uneasy, and yet God wants you to know that shalom is coming. It has already been won at great cost, and it *is* coming. It's unstoppable. It's unspeakable. It's incomprehensible. Yes, please do go in the name and the strength of the Lord and give expression to it today – feed the hungry, clothe the naked, give water to the thirsty and visit the prisoner. And take a meal to your sick neighbour, offer to babysit for a frazzled single parent, give someone you know who is in need a generous gift.

Take a moment to consider how you can share the peace of God with someone today.

Be a peacemaker.

Notes

1   Henri Blocher, *In the Beginning* (IVP, 1984), p. 15. Emphasis in original.
2   James Limburg, *Hosea-Micah* (John Knox Press, 1988), p. 186.
3   Harriet Sherwood, 'Nearly 50% are of no religion – but has UK hit "peak secular"?', *The Observer*, 14 May 2017, **theguardian.com/ world/2017/may/13/uk-losing-faith-religion-young-reject-parents-beliefs**.
4   Shane Claiborne, Jonathan Wilson-Hartgrove and Enuma Okoro, *Common Prayer: A liturgy for ordinary radicals* (Zondervan, 2010), p. 382.
5   Stella Simiyu, quoted in Dave Bookless, *Planetwise* (IVP, 2008), Appendix Question 6. For more information on A Rocha, see **arocha.org**.
6   See Saul McLeod, 'Maslow's hierarchy of needs', **simplypsychology. org/maslow.html**.
7   Department for Business, Energy and Industrial Strategy, 'Government reaffirms commitment to lead the world in cost-effective clean growth', press release, 12 October 2017, **gov.uk/government/ news/government-reaffirms-commitment-to-lead-the-world-in-cost-effective-clean-growth**.
8   One of the best books on this subject is by Preston Sprinkle, William Loader, Megan K. DeFranza, Wesley Hill and Stephen Holmes, *Two Views on Homosexuality, the Bible and the Church* (Zondervan, 2016). See especially the section by Stephen Holmes entitled, 'What space is there for pastoral accommodation in this area?' (p. 190).